Threefold Cord and Incredible People

This book is also available online at
www.thegift.org.uk

Ann Nunn
Assisted by Liz Leach Murphy

Kingdom Publishers

The Gift
Copyright© Ann Nunn

All Scripture Quotations have been taken from the New International Version and the King James Version of the Bible.

ISBN: 978-1-913247-67-6

1st Edition by Kingdom Publishers
Kingdom Publishers
London, UK.

You can purchase copies of this book from any leading bookstore or email
contact@kingdompublishers.co.uk

Thanks to

Liz Leach Murphy, Jayna Patel, Mollie Williams, Celia Stone, Sam Denison, Barbara Binder, Alan and Angela Clarke, Stephanie Thompson, Ali Marsland of Effective English Company for proof reading, to all the members of Simons Circle of Support - 'Full Steam Ahead', to Church on the Way in Idle, Jim King and David Barlow. Esme Stott Leach, Rufus Stott Leach

Dedication

Dedicated to my Dearly Beloved Peter

Preface

One day in around 1969, we were in the kitchen, having just returned from a family shop with boxes of groceries scattered all around the room, when I noticed Simon sitting on the kitchen floor studying the writing on the side of a box; he was interested and perplexed by the marks he could see.

It was then that I realised that Simon was studying all those markings and trying to work out their meaning. This was the beginning of a tremendous breakthrough in my mind.

Content

The Gift

I have always believed that people are full of potential and latent skills, I have strived to create relationships with people where they feel able to flourish and feel supported in what they decide to do and this is exactly the type of relationship I forged with my son.

Simon is the inspiration for writing this book.

When Simon was young and keen to learn he challenged me and his father, Peter, to consider different ways that he could engage in learning. Until that time, we had not considered teaching Simon and how we would approach teaching him. We had been doing drawings of his favourite things – lorries and tractors – as a way to entertain Simon, but not with the intention of teaching him. He would show interest in the boxes in the kitchen, trying to make sense of the writing on their packaging. We knew we had to find a way that he enjoyed.

Simon was born in 1965 and he was diagnosed with a condition called cri du chat when he was two years old. He was also diagnosed with autism much later in life in the mid-1990s, when he was in his 30s.

> "Cri du chat is a rare genetic disorder caused by a deletion in the short arm of chromosome 5. This disorder is also referred to as 5p- syndrome. The condition affects an estimated 1 in 50,000 live births and strikes all ethnicities."

> Cri Du Chat / 5p- Syndrome, 2011

The cri du chat support website provides further information about the condition including a list of symptoms. Here are some of the physical symptoms of cri du chat that Simon experiences:

- A cry that is high-pitched and cat-like
- Fine motor delays
- Speech and language delays
- Constipation
- Sleeplessness

    Cognitive delays – for Simon this would depend on the subject and how interested he was in it. He can be very quick when he is keen on the subject.

Other symptoms of cri du chat that Simon doesn't experience include:

- Small head circumference (microcephaly)
- Small jaw (micrognathia)
- Wide-set eyes
- Skin tags
- Partial webbing or fusing of fingers or toes

There are more symptoms of the condition that people experience, and it affects people in different ways. More information can be found on the Five P Minus Society's website at http://fivepminus.org/.

People diagnosed with cri du chat *'will likely need a lifetime of support.'* (Five P Minus Society, 2016).

From a young age Simon was seen as "different", and this is when our challenges began. Communication was one of the biggest challenges. His appearance made him stand out from the crowd and attract attention and his level of dependency was much higher than other children his age. He would always need either me or his Dad close by.

We embraced the challenge and did everything we could to support Simon to learn. To our delight, Simon is now an adult and living life to the full. He is able to do much more than anyone ever expected. He has a photographic memory; he remembers everything he reads and sees and if you want to know anything you just need to ask him – providing it is of interest to him. Simon uses a computer, attends steam fairs, attends interesting courses about history (e.g. the Plantagenets) and industrial developments and goes on fun but also informative outings. Simon either travels on the bus with his support worker or by car. We are still committed to teaching Simon as much as we can.

Teaching Simon has been such a lovely experience and we have kept all our teaching materials and books that we made together.

One day I had the thought: *'I wonder if someone else would benefit from these teaching materials and the books that Simon and I made?'* I took some of the books that Simon and I had created to our church pastor, Lee, who said: *'You shouldn't keep these in your handbag Ann, they could be of tremendous worth and a treasure for many people. You could help people all over the world with their child'.*

The first signs of study and interest

One day in around 1969, we were in the kitchen, having just returned from a family shop with boxes of groceries scattered all around the room, when I noticed Simon sitting on the kitchen floor studying the writing on the side of a box; he was interested and perplexed by the marks he could see.

It was then that I realised that Simon was studying all those markings and trying to work out their meaning. This was the beginning of a tremendous breakthrough in my mind.

When we realised Simon wanted to learn

By this time Simon was aged four and he had not been developing and reaching the milestones of development that we had expected, including the milestones associated with maintaining eye contact, sleeping, diet, routines, behaviour and socialising. Simon didn't walk until he was four years old. His language also wasn't developing well, and this made it difficult to communicate with him.

We had tried words, articulation and concepts, although Simon was not remembering and making use of these. Peter and I had firmly believed he understood everything (he would show eagerness and receptiveness and respond enthusiastically when we tried to teach him something new or introduce a new word), but he found it more difficult to express himself. He never showed any signs of becoming frustrated about this, and together we found a way for Simon to begin to express himself and we began to understand each other. For instance, sometimes Simon would contribute to a conversation by finding a toy or a picture that was relevant to the conversation and what he wanted to contribute to it.

From that moment with Simon and the box in the kitchen onwards, Peter and I committed ourselves to teaching Simon and supporting him to realise his potential through developing his natural curiosity and interest.

A ridiculous suggestion

Once we had started to engage Simon in activities to support him to learn, Peter asked if I could teach Simon to read. At that time, it seemed like a ridiculous suggestion and I didn't know where to begin.

How could I teach my son to read? I had not been trained as a teacher; I had been trained to be a nurse. Where was I supposed to start? How was I supposed to do this?

I didn't have a clue what I was doing. I was overwhelmed, and the increased sense of responsibility was enormous. I thought at length about how to approach teaching Simon, but I asked the Lord to show me what to do and how to teach Simon.

So where did I start?

I started by spending time with Simon painting pictures of his favourite subjects.

When we first started, I was not a good artist (see illustration) but to compensate, I wrote names on the drawings to go with the image to give Simon a clue.

this makes the road flat

The Teaching book

One day I was out shopping, and I saw a book in the local shop entitled *"Teaching Reading"*. I bought the book and I had to decide whether to follow the plan set out in the book, or whether to ask the Lord to show me the way.

I decided to let Jesus show me the way, but I did use the word list at the end of the teaching book, which gave the order in which words should be taught.

The alphabet

After a while we began to have an alphabet letter a day with pictures of Simon's favourite things beginning with that letter.

After two years we had reached the last of the suggested teaching words on the list at the "normal" time for any school child. It was a fantastic achievement, especially for someone who had been deemed impossible to educate and who had been taught by someone who had no training in teaching, but the Lord is the best teacher!

The gallery

At the time we started to teach Simon he was waking at 3am and tearing wallpaper off the walls. He was ripping up sheets, books and bedsheets and slithering down the stairs.

This sounds destructive, but the surprising thing is, when he was tearing things up, I was glad that he was! This feeling took me by surprise, but before then he had not done anything at all, and this was the first thing he had started to do using his own initiative. I then recognised that Simon had an intention to do something and it was my role to support him to focus his attention on something positive and productive.

I decided to put the pictures we had created to illustrate the alphabet letters up on his bedroom wall; I needed to do something with them rather than them being in a book. Each time we completed a picture we would add this to his gallery that was forming in the hope that this would distract him from his destructive and disruptive behaviour.

He took great joy in his pictures. It was successful, and it was the start of Simon really beginning to learn. His gallery was the beginning of a period of wonder, excitement and discovery.

He started to use letters to communicate and we realised that amazingly Simon had absorbed it all, everything we had taught him so far.

Adapting to continue the teaching

After finishing the suggested teaching word list at the end of the Ladybird book, we began working in exercise books rather than on sheets of paper and we called these schoolbooks "fun books". We started on "fun book" no. 1 when Simon was six and ¾ years old. The "fun books" included anything that Simon found interesting and fun. As well as new knowledge, each of these books were full of pictures of Simon's favourite things with text to go with them. The content of these brown paper books covered a broad range of subjects, including fruits, different countries, farming and languages. We used a blackboard easel as well as the brown paper books and often learnt a lot simply by talking to many enthusiasts on subjects they knew a lot about.

Authorities and negativity

When Simon was between the ages of two and 10 years old, we had no contact with the local authorities. At the time we were of the opinion that if we got involved with the local authority, we would have a battle to keep Simon in our lives as they would recommend that Simon be based in a long-stay hospital, which was the way things tended to be in the 1960s and 70s. We felt they really would take control, meaning we would struggle to maintain our sense of control over our lives. We thought that we would have to battle against all their negativity and their focus would be on what was "wrong" with Simon and on identifying ways that Simon's problems could be fixed, thinking and assuming that they knew best.

The practice of the local authority at this time was to put everyone with a learning disability into the same place in day centres, residential care units or hospitals, in essence, large institutions. The professionals were more often than not of the opinion that this would be a good outcome for the person and their family. People often heard phrases like: *'he'll be better there'* or *'he'll be safe there; you can get on with your lives; you can always try for another child'*. However, just because a person has a learning disability it does not mean that they only want to spend time with other people with learning disabilities. Simon wanted to spend time with people who shared the same interests and had a similar sense of humour and he wished to be with his family, be in the community and go to church. He was a free spirit (and still is) and one who did not want to be confined.

Before the age of 10, Simon had been home schooled. That had been our choice as we believed that there were no schools that could cater for Simon's needs or that could provide Simon with an adequate opportunity to learn. We were also afraid to draw attention to ourselves and our situation by being involved with a school because we were afraid of Social Services. We knew what the thinking and approach to families in our situation was back then and were understandably wary. We were subsequently proved correct.

Educational psychologist

During Simon's younger years Peter's dad had become desperate with the commotion in our lives that had resulted from us being jobless and homeless and felt that it needed sorting out. He arranged a visit from an educational psychologist when Simon was 10 years old, believing that this would bring some solutions and a sense of order to our lives.

The educational psychologist was called Mrs Smith. We had a number of meetings with her and, although Peter and I had informed her of our approach to educating Simon, she immediately reached the conclusion that Simon was not able to learn and had not learnt any of the skills we professed to have taught him. At this stage she had formed this opinion simply by observing Simon, but she had not engaged him in any meaningful activities to be able to assess him thoroughly. She had been making incorrect assumptions.

She certainly didn't believe in Simon's success in learning to read; for her it was a forgone conclusion: Simon had learning disabilities and was uneducable.

To prove the point during one of her first visits to the family home, I wrote a message on a piece of paper for Simon: *'Please go and fetch an orange for me'*. I folded this up and gave it to Simon so that Mrs Smith could not see what was on the paper. Simon left the living room and went into the kitchen and came back to me with an orange. I asked Simon to pass the piece of paper to Mrs Smith who, upon unfolding the piece of paper and reading it, was flabbergasted. She was eager to know and understand more about how Simon had been educated and from that point onwards we had a very good relationship. At this stage Mrs Smith started to engage with Simon more and began to assess his learning and his scope to learn. These tests resulted in Simon demonstrating a much higher level of understanding than she had originally expected and that he did have a capacity to learn.

Keeping up appearances

When Peter was first admitted to a psychiatric hospital (see chapter called *"Us - A Threefold Cord"* for more on this part of our life), the local authorities were notified and made aware of our existence and our circumstances so we had to play it their way because we were no longer in command of our situation. Therefore, after the involvement from the educational psychologist, we were put under pressure to send Simon to school against better judgement.

To keep the education authority happy, Simon started to put in an appearance at a local school. In 1975, Simon began attending Stanstead School, a special school, three mornings a week. Peter and I really struggled with this decision as we knew it would be a holding place for Simon, that he wouldn't gain a great deal from going there and he would learn much, much more if we were able to continue to teach him at home through the day.

Limiting schooling

When we visited, we learnt that Stanstead School didn't have any mind-stretching reading material. All the books were for nursery children and these were not of any interest to Simon.

The school was incapable of engaging Simon's interests and the material they had available was not going to encourage him to expand his ability to read. All the youngsters at the school were below the age of 10 and had learning disabilities. Neither the teachers, nor the school, had vision for the children who attended, and they had no aspiration for them or belief that the pupils could attain any more than what was expected of them.

The school provided no one-to-one time to dedicate focused attention to each pupil; it was a very small setting that did not offer any aspiration for the young people who attended, with no out-of-school visits to beneficial places such as museums.

I visited the school one sunny day and the teachers were kind to me. However, when I spoke to Simon's teacher and the assistants about my hopes for Simon and his future it seemed as if they did not understand his potential or his educational needs. They demonstrated little knowledge regarding how to teach pupils to read and had no intention of doing so. They had no awareness of Simon's capabilities and how to support him to achieve as much as possible whilst in school.

When I shared the approach I had taken to teach Simon how to read, they were quite interested in the techniques and tactics I had used but unfortunately they said that they didn't have the time to provide one-to-one tuition and therefore, could not follow this approach in the school.

As a visitor I could see that it would have been possible if they had the vision and the motivation to do so. They had the capacity to embrace a one-to-one approach to teaching for at least some of the school day as there were approximately 15 pupils and five workers.

The school had lots of children with completely unrealised potential. They needed to be supported and given focused one-to-one education. Instead, the teacher would gather all the children to sit around a table, so she could read to them, but no books would be given to the children to allow them to follow along with what she was reading. Unsurprisingly, just as the teacher was about to begin, Simon would get up and go and fetch his own book. He wouldn't take part in a reading group that required him to listen; Simon wanted to read himself and learn.

Limited interaction with his peers

Simon did not have a lot of interaction with the other pupils at the school and was not gaining anything from this socially or academically. After observing Simon at school, the educational psychologist recognised that it really wasn't doing him any good, but she had to go along with the arrangement due to her professional role and duty to play "the game".

The journey to school

When Simon started at school, we lived in the countryside and our home was a long drive away from the school. To help, two volunteers supported and drove Simon to school. After a little while, Peter and I started to have doubts about the taxi volunteers. Over time, we realised that we had begun to dislike them more and more; they were horrible, unpleasant and patronising and they had a bad attitude. When Simon was sat in the taxi, they didn't speak to him nicely, their subjects of conversation were unpleasant, and we felt they were condescending towards us all. Simon told us that he felt the same way; he became distressed at the thought of having to spend time with the volunteers and he really did not look forward to the journeys to school; he was always pleased to be home and each morning we had to persuade him to go. Eventually this dislike became mutual and, after Simon had attended school for just two months, one day, without providing us with an explanation, the volunteers said they wouldn't be doing it anymore. What a huge relief!

Back to home schooling

At the time we did not own a vehicle, we did not have access to transport and there was no public transport route from our home to the school. The school was 20 miles away from our home, far too far for us to walk with Simon. Therefore, Simon did not have transport to get to school. The education authority tried to find more volunteers, but no-one came forward. When the barriers to actually getting to school became clear, the education authority decided that he didn't need to go any more – meaning we could return to home schooling. We were all over the moon. Simon settled and was less distressed; he started learning much more again.

After this experience the authorities left us alone and I continued with Simon's daily lessons, which we had kept doing whilst he was at school.

What materials do you need?

You do not need a lot of expensive materials to be able to start to teach someone. I taught Simon during periods of our life where we had nothing, and we were homeless due to being jobless and having no income. So please do not let a lack of resources, or not having the latest technology, be the reason you don't give this a go. We were resourceful and made use of anything we had available to us. I would keep anything that I thought could become useful.

Whatever our circumstances I always tried to carry a notebook and pens with me so we could capture moments where the opportunity for learning arose.

I realised that we needed reading books; these were essential. I would collect them from charity shops, or loan them from the library and sometimes friends would give me books that they thought would be useful. Strickland Gillian's poem *"The Reading Mother"* was always a favourite of mine for perfectly illustrating the wonder of learning that can be unlocked when a parent reads to a young child.

> *'You may have tangible wealth untold;*
> *Baskets of jewels and coffers of gold.*
> *Richer than I you never can be --*
> *I had a mother who read to me.'*

During the early stages of Simon's learning when he was about five, we had a blackboard and easel. We kept this in the kitchen, and we would use it to write or draw anything we had on our minds. For example, if we had heard the weather forecast or the news we would write and illustrate it, or if a friend had visited, we would illustrate the conversations we had had.

People: The greatest resource

People were one of our biggest resources and, by taking the time to talk to people, we would learn so much.

We would talk to people when we were out and about and one day, we got talking to a man who was digging drainage trenches in a field. He collected old glass bottles, and by chatting to him we found out so much about road working, glass bottles, fossils and fossilised ganister!

Passions and interests

We would talk to people about their passions and interests. Firstly, we would find out what their interests and passions were and then we would talk about them. We always found that once we had discovered what an individual's interests were, they would be more than happy to talk at length about them and we would find out so much information.

We also made great use of libraries, galleries and museums and, when visiting places, we would take our time and enjoy the whole visit, reading all the information.

Routine

Even during times of isolation, desperation and poverty when we experienced homelessness and unemployment, we were still focused on educating Simon. We had a regular teaching session every afternoon and developed a routine that worked for Simon. Through this structure he got into the swing of learning.

Simon was immensely interested; he was talkative and consumed by what was going on. His level of curiosity and enthusiasm meant that I became very passionate about the learning process and Simon's response added to my motivation.

We had found a mutual eagerness to learn and teach, and this inspired and motivated me to become more confident in my teaching skills. It was fun and exciting, and it definitely wasn't a chore.

Letters to words to phrases

In our drive to teach Simon to read, we quickly progressed from letters to words and then subjects with simple phrases underneath with the word to be learnt highlighted.

Simon took the lead in his own learning as I drew. The time we spent together to learn and to teach was mutually rewarding, satisfying and stimulating.

This continued for two and half years, until we had used up all the teaching/reading words listed in the Teaching Reading book we had bought.

(Illustration 1.14)

Key Words
with Peter and Jane

These flash cards contain the 100 key words that scientific research has shown make up 50 per cent of those we read, write and speak every day.

The first twelve words in the chart below make up 25 per cent of those used. You can introduce these first to learner readers. Then proceed to the next 20, followed by the remaining 68 words

25%	a and he I in is it of that the to was
	all are as at be but for had have him his not on one said so they we with you
50%	about on bock been before big by call came can come could did do down first from get go has her here if into just like little look made make me more much must my new no now off old only or other our out over right see she some their them then there this two up want well went were what when where which who will your

Ensuring success with Key Words flash cards

Using Key Words flash cords helps children recall a word on sight, which in turn helps with reading, spelling and building sentences of their own. Children learn quickly when they are having fun Below are some tips for playing games with these cards.

- You can begin by selecting words important to your child, making your own cords if necessary These could include your child's name, the name of their pet or 'Mummy. Explain what the words say and talk about the letters and sounds Con your child recognise the words as you hold up the cords? Can he or she peck them out from a small group of other flash cards?

- When these words ore recognised, progress to another small group of cords

- Games help develop memory: you can use toys to help you mime position words such os in', 'on', 'up', 'down', 'over'. Can your child find the cord that says the word'"

- You can also use the cards to make short sentences together I om big/litlie_ it is old/new. We have one/two. You can see Peter and Jane doing this in book 4c

Time will tell

Over time my artistry improved, and I realised teaching Simon had also been an opportunity for me to learn and develop new skills (see the illustrations below).

on the shore

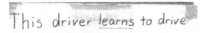

I became very confident in my newfound skills. I was always dedicated to teaching Simon, but I never realised how much I would enjoy it. The success was continually growing. Simon's knowledge developed each day and his ability to recognise and read letters, and eventually words, was clear to see.

We played a lot with words and Simon developed a love for word games.

box   pen   thing
fox   Ben   nothing
ox   den   something
of   fen   anything
wall   hen
all   men
ball   ten   mean   beans
call   then   bean   baked
fall   when   clean   black eye
hall   use   glean   green
tall   fuse-box   jeans   broad
tall   lean   butter
wall   wean
ink   fly   runner
drink   by   string
link   cry   french
pink   dry   dwarf
link   my
pink think why
pink sink

This made it fun and we still enjoy word play together now. We often have a bit of a giggle by rhyming words and merging words together to create a whole new word that only we know the meaning of.

Team effort

Although I spent a lot of time with Simon looking at letters and words, drawing pictures and teaching him how to read, this was a team effort between us all.

I led on the daily lessons with Simon but, we worked together as a family.

Peter got involved in the word games and he supported us with everything in every way. We had a set of plastic letters which Simon and Peter played with on the floor. They would take one sound and move the letters around to achieve the same sound to make words rhyme. It started with easy word games like "at" and creating "bat", "cat", "fat", "hat", "mat", "pat", "rat", "sat" and "vat" and then led onto more difficult ones like "there", "they're" and "their".

It was wonderful and exciting to see Simon's response to these games and it went on and on and got better and better.

New ideas

Peter and I talked about teaching Simon frequently and we enjoyed spending time together discussing it. Whilst talking, we would consider what Simon was enjoying and the areas he was progressing in.

I referred to Peter for support and guidance, especially when I was searching for some information or facts to teach Simon or seeking inspiration.

The conversations with Peter about Simon's teaching helped in so many ways. They opened up new ideas and possibilities about how to teach him. We talked about things to try and approaches to take. It provided the support we both needed to continue and move forward despite all the negativity surrounding us. We were, and still are, a very good team.

we brush our teeth up and down

give me the S.R. please

'We pick the fruit for jam

We want to get it before it falls'

Getting on board

When I started to teach Simon, he was already on board and eager to learn and find out more, which helped immensely. We were on the same wavelength, which, again helped as Simon was as keen as I was for him to learn.

Simon would show his understanding by going to get whatever it was we were talking about. For instance, if we were talking about planes he would go and get his toy Spitfire.

If there was something Simon wanted to learn he would tell me directly; he would show me by taking me to what it was he wanted to learn or by pointing it out in a book.

I cannot remember a time when Simon was ever bored; this was helped by us ensuring that Simon had the chance to learn in many different places, which involved us going out and about and visiting places of interest.

Also, he didn't get bored because I would say, *'only boring people get bored!'* I fundamentally believed there was too much of an abundance of places to see and visit, things to do and experience and topics to learn in the world for a person to ever be bored!

Inspiration is all around

We both appreciated that everything and anything around us could serve as valuable teaching materials. These everyday things included roadworks, museums, weather forecasts, people and the news. We would point things out to Simon and draw his attention to what was taking place in his surroundings. We would explain things to him or, if there were people, such as curators, farmers or workmen, doing the work, we would ask them to explain what they were doing.

Workmen

Simon has always had an interest in workmen. Whenever workmen come to our home Simon's first act is to put a traction engine in place to "assist the men with power". After the work is complete, he needs a piece of wood or pipe etc. from the workmen as this enriches his play experience.

Anything mechanical

With Peter's help, Simon developed an excellent understanding of all things mechanical. After all, since Peter is a trained and educated engineer and both Peter and I had engineers as parents or grandparents, it was "in the blood". For example, Simon learnt how a car or steam traction engine works. We taught him by studying diagrams, looking under car bonnets and at stripped down steam engines and listening and chatting to the engine enthusiasts whilst they were on the job – people with their heads under car bonnets, who tinkered with the back of the organ and who worked inside engine workshops doing the greasy, dirty, fiddly and intricate jobs.

Learning to mix, or not!

Simon reached a stage in his development at which I felt he should have the opportunity to learn to share and mix.

Not having the opportunity to go to school did have its drawbacks and I encouraged Simon to spend more time with other people, especially children of his own age. During this time, Simon did learn how to mix and share to a degree, but this was very difficult for him and often he would not share or mix at all.

There also weren't many opportunities for Simon to mix with people his own age. When we lived at Allerton in Bradford he would not play outside with others, he had no cousins who lived close by or who were close in age and when he attended Stanstead School he was more likely to approach a teacher or adult than one of his peers. When the rare chance did arise for Simon to mix with people his own age, he would initiate contact with another child, but the child would often not know how to respond to Simon. I think maybe his contemporaries couldn't understand how someone who was so like them was also so different and strange. However, with some assistance and encouragement, Simon and the child he was mixing with could find things in common.

I believe that Simon's unwillingness/inability to mix and share was due to him having autism and therefore he had his own unique perspective of the world and his own way to engage with people.

Teaching under difficult circumstances

Teaching was a challenge that I took on board, but we had personal challenges along the way which added to the complexity that we had to work around. We had times when our finances were really not so good, where our home life was unsettled and when we were homeless (see chapter titled *"Us - A Threefold Cord"*).

We experienced the negative attitudes of other people and had to cope with the effects of this. The teachers that we knew did not regard Simon as someone who could be educated. My aunt was a teacher and she said that Simon would, *'never amount to anything'*.

At the time we finished the suggested list in the Teaching Reading book we had become homeless. We did not let this hold us back and we continued teaching and learning together, developing Simon's reading, writing and understanding.

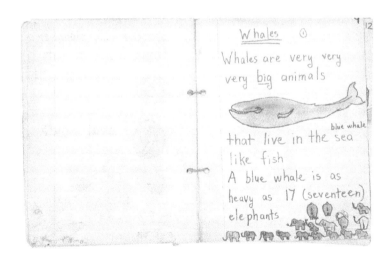

Book Two

Simon just felt like having a picture
of a prime mover with a bull dozer
Because it is a long vehicle, we had to
go long ways

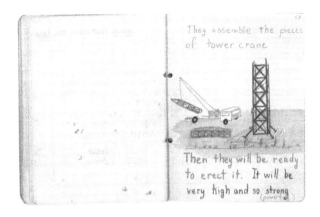

At this stage we were staying in Exeter for a few weeks and the "fun book" we were working on at the time captured what we did together when we lived there, including collecting fossils from the beach and watching building sites develop.

We made time to teach Simon whilst also going out and trying to find a place to live. This multitasking was distressing and at times, unpleasant but for Simon's sake, we kept up our front of being calm and reassuring.

Lasting distress

Despite still managing to dedicate time to teaching Simon, time we all enjoyed, this period in our lives was, at times, very distressing; and this distress left a lasting mark. When Simon looks at the books from this time he will say, 'not now'. *The books do a brilliant job at capturing all the good times. There were, however, bad times but these were recorded on pages that have since been removed from the original books and destroyed as both Peter and Simon find these memories difficult to cope with.* Although the books capture all the good days, on the pages that have been removed all the bad times are captured and both Peter and Simon can find these memories difficult to cope with.

During these stressful times Simon and I would sometimes need to get away, so we would take small notebooks with us and record everything about what we were seeing and experiencing.

Before Simon was 10 years old between 1973 and 1975 whilst we were still homeless, we stayed in Castle Hedingham. During this time Simon and I did a lot of truck spotting and watching combine harvesters. We also investigated factories, explored disused railway lines and sat observing trees, woodland and much more.

Peter's dad supplied *Farmers Weekly* as a source of inspiration and to this day it remains a favourite weekly magazine for Simon.

We spent time writing about many things, including Louisiana, where we had a friend, Ben, and we learnt about so many other countries.

How the "fun books" developed

Despite our fluctuating living situation and the distressing experiences we had endured, we were determined to continue to help Simon develop and learn. By May 1974 we had started on "fun book" no. 15.

This illustrated farms, including sheep, barns, and machinery. We also covered Brazil, various other countries, owls and deer and sat and observed the trees and woods. We did leaf rubbings and researched and learnt about Dutch elm disease, nature and feathers!

We also tried to do numbers, but neither of us was very good at them. There were plenty of combine harvesters about to enjoy and delight in instead!

The countryside was beautiful, especially the picturesque duck pond at Finchingfield and there were many windmills to admire.

Mother's book

In 1974 we moved to Dorset and lived there for a short while. There, I continued to teach Simon.

I had started to keep a "mother's book" in which I kept a record of the subjects we had looked at together. This was separated into different subject headings including: reading, writing, arithmetic, scripture, nature, history, geography, French and colouring.

Here I listed everything we had learnt, and it was my personal record of what we had done and ideas for future learning. The subjects we had covered were extensive, fun and interesting.

Carrying on the learning amidst the chaos

We certainly had our share of difficult times. As we were on the move a great deal and unsettled, due to becoming homeless in the early seventies after receiving an exceptionally high rates bill that we could not afford to pay (see the chapter entitled *"Us – A Threefold Cord"* for further explanation), we had to become far more organised. We were still very poor, and we could not afford very expensive workbooks.

The larger books were made of brown paper and in these books we talked about farming, French, geography, art and many other subjects.

When Simon had learnt to read, I went back to look at the Teaching Reading book we had bought and I found, to my amazement, that I had used the two methods suggested, i.e. phonetics and word recognition.

Stepping up a gear

Once Simon had developed his confidence and ability to read, we progressed onto more complex levels of learning and we made use of our main textbooks on the subjects of geography and nature.

I continued to teach Simon up to the age of 19.

When Simon reached the age of 20, we made the decision to start scrapbooks and move away from the "fun books".

We wrote anything down that came into our minds into the scrapbooks, anything that we would see at home or when we were out and about. If we were staying anywhere for a long time it was useful to have a notebook to make notes that we could transfer into the scrapbooks when we got home. We would also pick up leaflets when we visited new places and take photos, transferring these into the scrapbooks upon our return home too. Simon liked to watch me writing about what we had done or seen that day.

Attending school

When Simon was 20, he started to attend High Trees School. The school and the teachers were fantastic, and they thought Simon was brilliant. Simon's friend, Mandy, also attended the school, and Andrea Brown was a very popular course tutor there.

This was a lovely experience and the first time we had felt any confidence in the education system. Simon attended this school for 18 months.

Eager to move

After attending school, Simon went onto a personal and community skills course. He loved this and did the course for 18 months. It was based at Joseph Nutter House and the course was led by Andrea. Simon had many friends at Joseph Nutter and his best friend was Sophia. During this course all the students were told that at some point during the course they would be moving school. Sometime after this announcement, the staff couldn't find Sophia or Simon anywhere. Eventually they found them; they were on the bus waiting to move school!

Simon also experienced his first journey abroad without Peter and me whilst on the course. As a group they went to Holland by ferry. Whilst everyone else was at the disco on deck, Simon and Andrea, the tutor who moved with Simon from High Trees School, were in the engine room with the captain inspecting, admiring and discussing the engine!

The personal and community skills course was brilliant for Simon. There were ten students on the course, all in their early 20s, and together they learnt about going to the bank, going shopping and everyday skills and also what was deemed as socially acceptable in all these settings. Most importantly, they had a lot of fun. Simon enjoyed it very much and he looked forward to going to his course. Unfortunately, the following year this course was closed for all the students, and all future students, who would have gained so much from it. The closure was on the pretext of modernisation. This was upsetting for everyone involved.

When Simon started to attend a day centre

Simon was in his mid-twenties when he started to attend day services. At this stage it was clear that Simon did not fit in at the services he was attending, and I was quite sure that they did not know how to support him well.

We started to use communication books when Simon started to go to different places, especially when he started to attend a day centre. It was a way of sharing information between us and Simon's support staff. The communication books captured what Simon had done that day and Simon could then share that with Peter and me when he came home. It gave us something to talk about and meant that Peter and I had an insight into how Simon had been spending his time and what was working well for him and, likewise, we could communicate with people back at the centre.

Here are some of the notes that came home with Simon in his communication book:

March 1999: *Made a hole in the newly painted wall by chipping at the plaster with a model plane. No reason. Has apologised.*

April 1999: *Scattering maps, reluctant to tidy*

May 1999: *Uncooperative and demanding at times*

June 1999: *Problems with picking*

August 1999: *Bored and unhappy*

September 1999: *Had the hood off someone else's coat and has left a rip*

December 1999: *Bitten on the hand by another member*

January 2000: *Problem with Simon putting his arm in another member's mouth and he got bitten. Needs supervision when moving around the building and at change-over times.*

March 2000: Simon has been lovely today, and a pleasure to be with. He collected the milk from the coffee bar. He knew where to go and asked for what he wanted.

Simon then moved to another day centre. He moved from Shipley to Legrams Day Centre in the hope that he would prefer Legrams and that he would get along better there.

Here are some notes from Legrams:

March 2001: Simon worked well; good concentration

July 2001: Simon unhappy all day

September 2001: Refused to take coat off; poor day. Good progress in other ways. Messy over lunchtime. Worked happily.

Although Simon found a good friend at Legrams, he did not fit in there either – there was always a problem. In all honesty, Simon likes to have the freedom to do his own thing and follow his own interests; this is how we had brought him up and how we functioned as a family so to expect him to fit in with an activity or a pre-arranged structured routine was largely alien to him.

As you can see, the majority of the feedback we received was negative and this was very difficult to digest when we had concentrated the majority of our time on encouraging Simon to feel positive about himself and encouraging the people around Simon to do the same. Can you imagine what it would be like if you constantly heard negative things about someone you loved dearly?

At this stage Simon had not yet been diagnosed as autistic and was therefore just a "troublemaker" for staff who were under pressure. Since this time, I have had chance to read the service review documents, which capture the opinions and concerns of the support staff who worked with Simon, and their approach seemed very unsafe and old-fashioned.

When Simon attended Legrams Day Centre he was taught by Sam Jackson, with whom Simon had a great relationship and he had the chance to really polish his computer skills and wrote a lot of interesting and entertaining stuff all about steam engines and what he saw when he was people-watching at the centre.

At a later stage, we achieved a grant to be able to purchase a computer to have at home to give Simon the opportunity to practice his computer skills. Simon loved to use his computer, which he called his "rumour machine" because he wrote outrageous stories about people and events.

He had developed his ability to type and spell words on the computer and he had become a dab hand at writing his own stories, which he called "rumours".

As Simon has got older he has put the skills he learnt into practice, he went onto write his own stories.

Education – the method

Teaching your child

The following sounds incredibly complicated but it's not. When you are teaching your child, focus on getting to a point where it is a pleasure. It will then become something you both look forward to.

Be completely engrossed with the experience and try not to be distracted by other thoughts or anything going on around you; make it clear to your child that they have your full attention and then you are likely to get theirs.

Be open to the idea that this is also an opportunity for you to learn as well as your child – you might even end up learning as much as them!

A small checklist

Here is a list of tips to keep in mind, which would be beneficial to implement when you are teaching:

- Aim to get to the point where teaching your child is a pleasure for you both.
- Communicate your own enthusiasm.
- Plan together what you will do – think about your aspirations, ambitions and dreams. Then work together towards achieving them.
- Be totally engrossed and try not to be distracted by other thoughts or anything going on around you.
- Recognise that you have as much to learn as you have to give.
- Have all the materials you need to hand and be prepared.
- Unleash your creative side; embrace painting and drawing etc.
- Be open and responsive to ideas and new things to try.
- Talk to people, who are a fabulous source of information, knowledge and enthusiasm.
- Be prepared to try different approaches.
- Get out and go to places; visit the places where you find useful information.

Make a plan of action

I always spent a bit of time planning with the aim of creating a routine. This helped me a great deal as it reduced a bit of the chaos and relieved the pressure.

Here is an example of our teaching programme over one week when Simon was nine years old:

Monday

1. Read *"Car Workers"* – with the aim to learn more about mechanics.

2. "Little pig" shops – the goal here was to learn maths and about handling money. I tried to make maths/arithmetic into a game, but it was not popular, and we were not very good at it!

3. Letter to Flyfield – this was a good chance to write a letter to my parents (using my hand to steady him).

4. Writing – with the aim of developing Simon's ability to write a letter.

5. French – pretending to shop with mother. The objective here was to master the basics of the French language and learn about the country's culture, which he did very well.

6. Looking at the world – the purpose of this activity was to build Simon's understanding of different countries, continents and flags.

Tuesday

1. Read *"Car Workers"* (aim as before).

2. Counting book 1+1 – we used our own counting notebook with the goal being to learn how to count and do basic sums.

3. Texts – the objective was to help Simon to learn to read.

4. Writing – to try and teach Simon to steady his hand and his letter shapes.

5. French – pretending to shop with mother (aim as before).

6. Look at the Bible – the purpose was to try to learn a psalm.

Wednesday

1. Read *"Car Workers"* (aim as before).

2. "Little pig" shops (aim as before).

3. Letter to our friends Gerome and Elise – with the purpose of giving Simon practice to steady his hand and work on his letter shapes.

4. Writing – to further develop the skills outlined in number 3.

5. French – "going to school in France" – the goal here was to learn about the French language and culture, which must have been the subject that we were concentrating on at the time.

6. Look at a book about nature – with the purpose of exploring the world around us.

Thursday

1. Read *"Car Workers"* (aim as before).

2. Counting book – the goal was to develop Simon's counting skills and ability to do basic sums.

3. Letter to Sophie (our niece and Simon's cousin) – with the purpose of nurturing Simon's ability and confidence in letter writing.

4. Writing – as above. The objective here was to assist Simon in steadying his hand while he wrote and to work towards improving his letter shapes.

5. Look at farm magazines – in order to develop Simon's understanding of farm animals.

Friday

1. Read *"Car Workers"* (aim as before).

2. "Little pig" shops (aim as before).

3. Letter to Canada or texts (aim as before).

4. Writing (aim as before).

5. French words related to cars – to learn fun facts about cars whilst developing French language skills.

How to create the plan

I would plan the teaching sessions using this approach:

Ideas – I would think through the subjects that would be good and interesting for Simon to learn.

Do – I would consider what we would need to do in order to learn about these subjects.

Get – I would ask myself: *'What do I need to teach these subjects?'*

Aim – I would establish what we aimed to learn.

For instance:

Ideas – Learn about the flags from all over the world.

Do – Create a geography scrapbook, and in it we can add images from magazines and draw pictures of countries and maps.

Go to the library to look at books. Reference an atlas and "Unstead" geography textbooks, which were designed for children.

Get – A scrapbook, some glue, magazines, scissors, a picture of the atlas, colouring pens and paper.

Aim – To recognise 10 flags and identify the country they represent and where the country is positioned in the atlas.

Planning in this way gave us the time to talk about what we were going to do and enabled us to have some structure and organisation to our approach. This helped Simon to know what to expect and gave me the opportunity to prepare for the teaching; in terms of timings, resources and the materials needed.

Why being flexible is a must

We never became too structured and unmovable. We were able to be flexible and responsive to Simon and his interests at any particular time as we realised that this was far more important than sticking rigidly to a plan and the results speak for themselves – it all went in. Simon absorbed everything we taught him! For us, to avoid our lessons being directionless and to keep us from floundering it was a case of having a balance – having a lesson plan but being careful not to treat the plan as if it was set in stone – be flexible with your plan!

The environment

Creating a stimulating environment that is conducive to learning is important and how you achieve this will be dependent on your child. The environment needs to suit their interests and include surroundings that make them comfortable and help them avoid distractions. Think about the light, the heating, the seating, background noise, the colours and the items you have to hand. In all these areas find what suits your child the most and make sure as much as possible, that the environment can offer a setting that is appropriate for your child; but just do your best in the situation in which you find yourselves.

Understanding autism

If your child has autism, learning about the condition and understanding the effects that autism has will help you appreciate how your child sees the world and interacts with it. Now that Simon is older there is a lot more information available and more awareness regarding autism than there was when he was younger. We must remember that not all people with autism are the same and it is essential that time is taken to determine what works for each individual – there is no blanket approach or way of managing the behaviour that results from autism as each person is unique.

Responding and understanding

For example, I developed an appreciation that, for Simon, the use of key words in his language was very important. This meant making sure that Simon understood and reacted to what was said to him quickly. For instance, if we needed to go and get the bus and I knew it was due soon it would be better for me to say:

'Let's go for the bus', rather than 'The bus is due; we must go now otherwise we will miss it'.

I would simplify my communication with Simon to avoid overload and confusion.

Simon's words – taken from Simon's World

The following is an extract taken from *Simon's World*, a very detailed and thorough document I compiled with Simon's support workers, friends and family at the recommendation of Simon's person-centred planning facilitator, containing all the knowledge I had about how best to care for and support Simon.

This is a collection of words and working phrases which are useful to know as Simon uses these on a regular basis and he really enjoys it and appreciates it if someone else uses his language.

Simon loves to play with words and enjoys word games e.g. changing a word slightly to make it sound different, for instance: "prayer feathers" – "prayer foothies" – "flithers" etc.

The words Simon chooses to use may not always stay the same and he will use different words with different people, personal to his relationship with them. For instance, only Simon and his mum, Ann, know what a "pobble" is and what a "twirley" is.

Here are examples of words and phrases:

- "Blip" – means we need to go to "plan B, C or D" etc or "change of plan".

- "Boak up" – Simon uses this word when something has gone wrong (this comes from the name of a person who runs a steam festival, and this quite often goes wrong). Always make sure when supporting Simon that if a "Boak up" happens there is a plan B in place. And always make something positive out of the situation.

- "Bothers" – when Simon mentions "bothers" he is referring to small things he can pick up from a charity shop for 50p or £1. This is something that Simon really enjoys.

- "Do the job properly" or "Get on with the job". This is something Ann says to Simon to encourage him to do the job properly.

- "Dropped the fusible plug" – when late or delayed.

- "Empty the fire box clinker" – to encourage to poo.

- "Exhibit" means don't touch (objects or people).

- "Feathers" – a very important word. It means lots of things. "Feather" can mean "good" or "lovely" but can also mean "my coat". When Simon goes out, he might be "feathering off".

- "A feather" is someone Simon likes.

- "Not a feather" or "fither" or "fulther" is probably someone he dislikes.
- "Feathery" means "really nice".
- "Be a feather" means "be good" – he tries to be a feather and needs praise.
- "Go for a quick feather" means go for a wee.
- "Come on feather" means "come on friend".
- "Feather off" means to depart/go/leave.
- "En feather" or "en wing" means hug.
- "Feathery feather" is a comment; high recommendation.
- "Feather" is also a word that he conjugates – it doesn't make sense, but it is fun.
- "Polish the brass" means clean teeth.
- "Luck", "magic" or "devil" – Simon doesn't like these words.
- "Rusty but trusty" refers to a heap of tatty old steam mags in the attic – useful if bored.
- "Strip and stuff" means remove his jacket and fold it away into his bag.
- "Swoose" is a combination of swan and a goose, but also a Second World War plane. Simon read a magazine about the plane and has adopted the word. Has used it for a while, but now he uses it as a word to conjugate. It also refers to birds.
- "Ugh" means "yuck" etc.
- "Wing Wings" – Simon's favourite toy is a wooden Showman's engine called Gabriel, driven by an angel called "Wing Wings" because she has two wings.
- "Vet" means a doctor or dentist.
- "Wing" – when Simon uses the word "wing" he is referring to a hand or arm.

My communication

Not all hand signals are insulting. I recognised the fact that hand signs could get through to Simon more effectively when his ears were too busy. Simon can be distracted and consumed by internal thoughts and sometimes he doesn't have space in his thinking to take on any external sounds like me talking to him, but he can respond to visual stimuli, e.g. hand gestures. I incorporated hand gestures into everything we did so that I effectively communicated with Simon even when he was in this preoccupied state, including whilst I was teaching him.

No television!

We had no television and no video games around when Simon was growing up and so we concentrated on everything going on around us. Everyday things, as well as places we visited and people we met. As Simon got older, he became more selective of the subjects he wanted to learn about and he chose history books, books about travel, fun books like the "Horrible Sciences" series, books on transportation and anything to do with steam, mechanics, windmills, organs and farming etc.

We continued to visit museums, a great source of interest for Simon, and he would go through them thoroughly, reading each section and taking it in and digesting all the knowledge that each museum and exhibit had to offer in detail. I remember often being in front of pictures at Cartwright Hall in Bradford and we would stand in front of them and critique them. We did this all the time at art shows and galleries, even if it was a plain brown canvas with a black frame – we weren't always very complimentary, but we had lots of fun!

A proud achievement

We still talk about how we taught Simon to read and we are proud of what we have achieved as a family and as a team.

We still reminisce about this amongst ourselves and with friends and family. We've kept all the "fun books" (all 145 of them!) and scrapbooks that are full of our teachings, learnings, exploring and adventures together.

Occasionally, we look at these together and they will bring back fond memories of the times we have shared. What should we do with them now? Any ideas?

A teacher friend

A friend of mine, Aliyah, was a teacher. She knew all about the approach we had taken to teaching Simon and she was overwhelmed by how well we had done and what Simon had achieved. She was jubilant that we had used "Unstead" books, geography textbooks for children, as a reference point in our teaching methods, in addition to listening, commenting and teaching based upon everything that came our way. She confirmed that we really had done a good job as teachers. This was very interesting, comforting and reassuring information!

The learning connection

Building a relationship with your child is THE main steppingstone in developing a connection that embraces learning.

My advice when helping your child along their journey to learn and grow is to make friends with them and become good buddies, understand their interests completely and help them to pursue their passions and hobbies.

Completely value your child.

If you feel a distance between the two of you, recognise what has caused the detachment and work to address this to bring you closer together. Pray about it if you can.

W.E.A. (Workers Education Authority)

Simon also returned to education much later on in life. In his late forties he attended some courses run by the W.E.A (Workers Education Authority) that he loved very much. One course was about the Last of the Plantagenets and another was about the gardens of Capability Brown, both subjects that Simon fully enjoyed and with which he was fully involved in the learning, asking questions and getting along with the tutor.

Simon's life now

Simon continues to often be misunderstood. One thing that is often not appreciated is Simon's level of intelligence, especially with anything related to engineering and steam. He has a photographic memory and is always inquisitive to read new information and learn new facts.

There are times when Simon uses complex words and, when people do not understand what Simon is saying, we may ask him to spell it.

At times when we still do not understand what Simon has said even after he has spelt it, we will write down the spelling together. Within context this is sometimes easier but if Simon mentions something out of context it can be more difficult. In these situations, Simon will find some reading material containing the word he is trying to communicate, or he will find the object. In these non-contextual cases it takes understanding and patience on both sides to correctly interpret what Simon is trying to convey.

Even now, it is vital that all the subjects covered are those that interest Simon, who can be focused and attentive on the subject being taught if it fascinates him. It is also important that Simon is with someone, such as someone from his circle of support (see page 20 of the chapter "Incredible People") or one of his advocates, who shares the same passion for learning and wholeheartedly believes he can learn so he can make real and meaningful friendships.

In my eyes, teaching Simon has been a joy, a pleasure and an exciting journey. Without his ability to read and communicate, Simon wouldn't be able to express what he wants to do and make important decisions about his life, such as where he wants to live, where he wants to spend time and who he wants to spend it with. Reading has also given Simon the confidence to maintain relationships with people at the church he attends and convey who he wishes to spend time with and how he wants to spend his time – usually with his fellow steam enthusiasts at steam fairs!

References

Cri Du Chat / 5p- Syndrome, 2011. About. [online] Available at: <https://www.facebook.com/pg/cdc.friendsofcriduchat/about/> [Accessed 30 April 2019].

Five P Minus Society, 2016. About 5P – Syndrome. [online] Available at: <https://fivepminus.org/about-5p-syndrome/#characteristics> [Accessed 30 April 2019].

A Threefold Cord:
A story of faith and triumph

I have faced many challenges in my life with surprising twists and turns, always with interesting outcomes. My faith is really important to me and my family, and God has been the provider of the strength I have needed at difficult times. The Lord has always been there for me. I know that Simon's future is in His safe hands. This is not easy, but I know (beyond all doubt) that GOD IS FAITHFUL.

Support

I attend a church fellowship on Tuesday evenings (bible class) and we are "family". We pray for each other and our concerns. This mutual support means a great deal to me.

I have also found great strength in loud singing, "songs of deliverance". These provide comfort and reassurance during difficult times.

In my times of desperation, I discovered for real that *'God is my refuge, strength and a very present help in trouble'* (Psalm 46:1), a constant support and companion. I am repeatedly helped, strengthened and comforted when I call on the name of the Lord to help.

Through believing in the Lord and believing in His promises I have felt comforted about Simon, what he can achieve and his future.

The hymn *"What a Friend we have in Jesus"* states: *'Take it to the Lord in prayer.'* (Hymnal.net, 2019a) and that is the best thing to do because we cannot cope on our own – but *'What a privilege'*! (Hymnal.net, 2019a).

This has given me a strength that has been invaluable, especially during times that have been very challenging when I have not been able to take the sorrows and burdens of the world upon me, but I have known who can.

My younger years

I was born in 1940 in Ilford, Essex at the beginning of the Second World War.

My happiest memories as a child include fishing in the pond for newts and frogs and visiting my grandparents who lived in the country. In those days, between the carefree ages of five and ten, I could wander through Epping forest on my own and I enjoyed looking for antlers. They were good times and I felt confident.

I have memories of the world events that took place as I was growing up – Queen Elizabeth II's coronation in 1953 and Churchill's 80th birthday in 1954.

As I became a little older, I began to keep bad company. I would spend time with girls who were going to nightclubs and sleeping around a bit. Their biggest ambition was to leave school as early as possible and go to work at Plesseys, the local electrical goods manufacturers.

Although we were at a grammar school together and really the sky was our limit; we could have aimed for anything. However, it was the norm at that time for girls and teachers to think small and do as their family had done before them. The height of my friends' ambitions was all that I also expected for my future.

When I was 14, I went on a trip to Paris with school which involved us each staying with a French family. We started study in the morning and sightseeing in the afternoon and this was a great way to learn French and see a new country and culture. Here I met a good friend who became a pen friend when I returned home.

In the late 1950s I was also expecting to have a straightforward life; meet someone, fall in love, get married and have a family. I had no grand plans for my far and distant future or a vision, just an expectation of what life would bring.

Turning point

At the age of 15 I went to a Whitsun Weekend Christian Conference. We enjoyed lots of fun and laughter. There was glorious sunshine all weekend. Our lectures took place on the lawns outside with the flower beds bursting with glorious blooms.

Our lecturer was McEwan Lawson, who was a lecturer in a congregational college speaking on the Holy Spirit. He was a kindly, gracious, wise old man leaning on the arm of his deck chair speaking with his eyes closed in the sunshine whilst we sat in the grass in front of him. I cannot remember anything that he said but I knew that I wanted what he was talking about more than anything in the world. I absorbed every word he said.

I likened this moment to being on a train line, going in one direction and someone changed the points. Suddenly I was heading off in a direction that I never expected, and I didn't understand what had happened.

My life and aspirations changed as a result of this experience. The scripture that captures this is: *'Therefore if any man be in Christ Jesus, he is a new creature'* (Corinthians. 5:17).

And in the words of *"Amazing Grace"*, *'How sweet the sound, That saved a wretch; like me! I once was lost, but now am found, was blind, but now I see.' (Hymnal.net, 2019b).*

At this stage it felt like my chains had fallen off. I felt that I understood the meaning of life.

A diary written in code

I knew that a big change had occurred in me and on my return home so did my family.

I didn't know what had happened to me and neither did my family, but I knew they would be searching my diary to find out, so I wrote in code to retain my privacy. How I wish I could read that diary now!

It was at this point that I knew that I must change churches. This was a huge thing to do especially as my parents where the pillar of the church which I had attended since being a child.

My parents were religious – congregational. I was the eldest of three so the one to bring the problems and challenges to my parents first, the first one to wear make-up, the first to go out, wear more daring clothes (which weren't very daring). My mum had a coat made for me and I refused to wear it. I wanted to wear fashionable clothes like trousers.

The relationship I had with my parents when I was at home had sometimes been tense. We didn't understand each other; we didn't argue, and we didn't have direct confrontation, but there was an underlying tension. We didn't have similar characters and we had different aspirations; that had always been the case. My mum wanted me to live the kind of life that she had lived, to continue my social life at their church, stay in the local area, maintain a close relationship with all my family and the people I had grown up with, meet a local boy from her church and settle down.

Family church

The church I went to as a child was a social church and much more open-minded than some but less spiritual.

I realised this was not right for me. I didn't have all the right answers. I didn't know how to respond in the way people expected and I didn't fit in. I wasn't a bad teenager, I wasn't uncontrollable, I just didn't feel comfortable in my own skin and I needed a place of worship that felt right.

At that time, I became very interested in the Roman Catholic faith and I sent off for a 21-week correspondence course. My parents were very distressed about this and every time I went home, they handed my post to me most reluctantly.

I had been very impressed by the film *The Nun's Story*, which was about Audrey Hepburn and her calling, novitiate and life as a nun. I guess that is why I wanted to investigate the Catholic faith. This was a short-lived interest which I did not pursue further after completing the correspondence course, but this did help me gain an insight and understanding into a different faith.

This reflects the type of person I am: open-minded, inquisitive and accepting of the views of others.

Much later in life, I saw *The Nun's Story* again and was so horrified that I turned it off. The horror of having to work one's way to redemption and salvation! They didn't know that there is a redeemer Jesus Christ the Lord – that the only way to salvation is to trust in his finished work as a free gift.

My future path

Before I left school, I had paid some thought to what future path I would like to pursue. I had reached the conclusion that I would either like to be a nurse or a prison officer. I shared these ideas with my mum to get her insight and perspective. My mum reacted strongly to these suggestions and whisked me off to the nearest nurse recruitment centre; she obviously could not stand the thought of me being a prison officer but was quite happy at the idea of me being a nurse.

Looking back, she did the right thing as nursing opened up a world of opportunity and I am sure that, without the nurse training I received, I would not have coped as well as I have done in meeting the care and support that my son, Simon, and husband, Peter, have required.

Cadet nursing

In 1957, at the age of 18, I was accepted as a cadet nurse at St Mary's Hospital in Paddington, central London. I was really looking forward to this opportunity. I was pleased that I had been accepted and my parents were also very proud.

I had some time to spare before the training would start at St Mary's, so I decided to use this time wisely and I went to work as a cadet nurse at their convalescent home in Oxford called Joyce Grove. The home had gorgeous grounds with sweeping cedar trees, violets in the grass, a walled garden and a little lake. My duties included dusting the elaborate panelling every morning and assisting the patients to get up, get to breakfast and to then go about their daily routines.

The house was "pseudo Jacobean". It was a lovely place and it was very grand. In the home there was one large men's ward, with about 12 beds. In this ward there was a huge carved oak fireplace and oak panelling all around. There were cherubs and bunches of grapes carved into the panelling. It was all very impressive. We had to dust the carvings every morning and our work was inspected to ensure it met the high standards expected.

At the far end of the building there were two female wards. The walls and ceilings of the wards were decorated with a mural of pretty paintings and gilding. In between these two wards was a very large hall and wide staircase all in dark wood. This was a huge space and part of this area was used as a dining room.

As nurses, our living quarters were in the attic, which was also lovely, comfortable and welcoming. I loved all the staircases and exploring the building; the roof was flat, and you could walk around up there amongst the very ornate chimneys. We often went up there, by climbing out of the windows and we would paint the view.

This was my first experience of being away from home, but I coped with it well. I had got to know people and there were four of us who were waiting to start the training at St Mary's, so we had a lot in common.

I caused a great excitement when I announced an intended trip to Paris. I had enjoyed my trip to Paris when I was 14 so much that I asked my pen friend if I could return to visit her. There was huge excitement amongst the staff team at Joyce Grove: "Nurse Hill is going to Paris!"

I travelled by plane, in an "old crate", across the channel. I am surprised we made it! I had such a great time when I got there and had plenty of stories to share when I returned. We went halfway up the Eiffel Tower and joyously ran all the way down the stairs and enjoyed lovely leisurely meals; where we sat talking at the dining table for hours and savoured many small portions whilst taking our time, carefree.

Nurse in training

I started 'preliminary' training at St Mary's Hospital between 1958 and 1962. St Mary's was one of the big London teaching hospitals based in Paddington, so it was prestigious and an exciting place to go.

This was the hospital where Alexander Fleming discovered penicillin and

Roger Bannister was a medical student at the time when he won the four-minute mile in 1954. This was a fantastic opportunity for me, and I really embraced it.

There was also a medical school adjacent to St Mary's and the medical students were being taught by the consultants based at the hospital.

St Mary's had sites all over the city and every three months student nurses would be allocated to a different ward to gain experience in different settings. During the time I was there these included a convalescence home in the country and Samaritans hospital for women on Marylebone Road alongside the Western Eye Hospital. We went on night duty for three months of the year while based at the nurses' home at Legrams Terrace in London.

We were moved about, from nurses' home to nurses' home, for different work experiences. We would pack all our possessions into a large trunk and move and settle into a new place on a very regular basis. Moving was not easy and even at that early age I was losing things. One night two junior nurses and I spent all our time searching high and low for the drug keys of the female medical ward. We searched in all the lockers, drawers and cupboards. Praise God we did eventually find them!

Study block

As part of our nursing training we had to complete "study block" sessions, which comprised six weeks of study in a classroom, where we didn't step foot onto a ward but when we were in study block, it was part of our duties to make the beds on various wards. We would turf patients out of bed before breakfast and then we would make all 40 beds before our breakfast. After that we would hurry down to the canteen where we had to answer to roll call, so that our superiors could check that all of us nurses were present and correct.

Every bed on the ward would get made twice a day in this manner. These were very neat beds, with hospital corners, all the castors turned the right way. The pillow openings turned away from the door. We performed this task with great precision; we had no idea we could make 40 beds in such a short space of time! It was a skill and I look back in wonder at how we performed the task so efficiently and fast.

For three months I was seconded to St Luke's Hospital, in London, a hospital for the dying. I worked there during 1959 and 1960. The staffs on the top floor were kind and compassionate but I was asked to work on the middle floor where the ward sister was wicked. She appeared to be taking and using the drugs in the ward drug cupboard. There were no rules and regulations then to govern this type of behaviour. She was unkind, cruel, unfeeling and hateful towards patients and staff. Her nursing standards were very low.

Whistleblowing

I decided I must try and do something about the ward sister's behaviour, and I went to the Matron of St Mary's Hospital to tell her. This may seem a fairly usual and expected course of action now but in those days, it was very unusual and unheard of, and no-one ever went to see the Matron.

Everyone perceived the Matron as too high in stature and position to even consider taking up her time. So, to get an interview with the Matron was an awesome experience and I went to tell her about the bad practice I had observed. This is now known as "whistleblowing" but at that time it was something people never did. I felt passionately about my role as a nurse and knew that this was a job that needed to be done well. I was disappointed and disillusioned by the response I received. The Matron was very dismissive and did not take my concerns seriously.

This was my first experience of "whistleblowing" and it shattered my confidence in the Matron.

At St Mary's, I had known I was surrounded by professionals who had high standards. I enjoyed my time there and felt I was part of something that was making a real difference, whereas at St Luke's I did not feel that people had the level of expertise, standards or professionalism that was needed. "Welcome to the real world!"

Merrydown

During my time as a trainee nurse at St Mary's, my friends and I would make time to have fun and we went out on a Saturday night; we just HAD to go to a "hop"!

I discovered that I wasn't very good at dancing or being social, but I found that the young men were interested in me when I said I was a nurse. They thought they were in for a good time. I tested this on one occasion by telling them I was a typist... they showed no interest in me at all!

A Saturday night wasn't complete without going to a "hop" and it was very popular. I discovered that medical students were a particular hazard – you had to beware of their motives and the "Merrydown" (a very potent cider)!

I did have many boyfriends and before I met Peter I had about five boyfriends at the same time and managed to keep them all platonic fairly well behaved.

Shame

The worst thing I did as a teenage student nurse was deciding to not pay the tube fair from Paddington and to take the chance at not being caught. At the time I was very short of cash, as we only got paid £20 a month and I didn't have money to pay for the train ticket. I was going to a church harvest supper with my grandfather and I really wanted to spend some time with him. This meant a journey by tube train from Paddington, central London to Ilford. On exiting the ticket barrier, I was asked for my ticket, and I acted blasé and said I had lost it.

The ticket man took my name and address and I knew I was in trouble; the experience was intimidating and frightening. When I arrived at the supper, I told my grandfather all about it and he was very concerned. A legal process began, and my father took me to a solicitor's office to discuss a way for him to manage the situation to get me off the hook. I was very relieved but more than that I was very shocked. I had been brought up not to lie and my father was now helping me when I had lied through my back teeth. After this, my family always tried to ensure that I had enough money so that I would not end up in the same situation again.

Many memories

There are many memories of my time at St Mary's. On one occasion a patient named Andras had fled the Hungarian revolution. He must have had no access to healthcare and was admitted to St Mary's Hospital with TB. Whilst there, he met and fell in love with a nurse (incidentally the same nurse who had supported me when I lost the ward drug cupboard key on night duty) and they married quickly. She was a good nurse but had to leave junior nurse training as this was the rule at the time.

Andras was successfully treated for TB but sadly did not recover. There was also cancer in his lung that had not been spotted on his X-ray. He lived for one month. His new wife stayed with him all the time and nursed him tenderly.

Completing our training

I continued diligently with my nurse training through the chaos and ups and downs. Whilst I was studying at St Mary's I was friendly with a group of nurses in my block and we went through all our training experience together, which included sharing accommodation. I often wonder where they are now... Where are you now Jo, Christine, Doris, Rosemary and Rachel? And how has life been since?

We all successfully completed our training in 1961. We were all set to become registered nurses and left St Mary's to get on with the rest of our lives, feeling that we were ready for whatever life would bring.

On completing my training, I was entitled to wear the Mary's Penny – bronze with inscriptions on each side. I was really proud of this achievement. I had worked hard, reliably and conscientiously to reach the standard of being a trained and registered nurse.

The Mary's Penny

I was looking forward to my career and putting everything I had learnt into practice, making a difference in people's lives when they were at their most vulnerable and ensuring that people felt truly cared for and respected. It was exciting.

Returning home

For a short while after qualifying I returned to live with my parents. I worked in a large mental health institution called Claybury Hospital which had at least 2,000 patients.

Claybury Hospital was in Woodford Bridge, Essex and it was first built in 1893, making it the fifth London County Council asylum. It was high on a hill and a great distance away from anywhere else. I had to get there early in the morning, and, with no form of satisfactory public transport, I decided to buy a second-hand Lambretta scooter, which behaved in a second-hand way! My dad used to get up early in the morning in his dressing gown and help me push the bike all the way up the road to get it started.

Moving from nurse training at St Mary's to Claybury Hospital was a huge culture shock for me; I had never seen or been in a hospital of that size before, caring for so many people. The place was so big you could use cycles in the corridors to get around.

Claybury Hospital catered for the whole district and therefore many people were sent to the hospital if they were suffering any form of mental distress, or for the numerous other unjust reasons people were sent to these institutions: women having children out of wedlock, post-natal depression, sexuality, to name but a few.

An eye opener?

In a lot of instances people did not require the hospital environment but, once in there, they found it very difficult to leave and, after some time, they must have resigned themselves to the idea that hospital was going to be their home for life.

When I started working there, I was needed on the infirmary ward because I was trained to do dressings and nursing care. Everyone else appeared to be untrained except the ward sister, who was mental health trained, but she spent all her time in her office. Doing what? The mind boggles.

I was gobsmacked by it all and I was busy trying to take it all in. I was young and newly trained, and I didn't really know how to respond. This was the first time I had worked in this kind of environment and I didn't really know what to expect, what was right and what was wrong. I knew that it didn't feel right and that the circumstances meant that I was not able to provide care or attention to the level that I would have hoped. There were 70 people on the infirmary ward alone and not enough carers. I was too naïve to know how to challenge this or that I could even challenge it. I tried to change practices at the hospital, and something must have gone in because I overheard an auxiliary nurse saying, "But Staff Nurse says that we must do it this way!" – They were referring to me!

I was shocked at how people living at the hospital had resigned themselves to the fact that it was going to be their lot in life and showed no fight or means to get themselves out of there. They had very few visitors and no contact with the outside world apart from the very rare visit out, so rare that one did not occur the whole time I was working there...months!

Patients were stuck within the hospital building for the majority of their time. I do not recall people having the opportunity to go outside, not even within the immediate grounds of the hospital. I can't remember the hospital having any gardens and no-one asked to go outside.

Patients often didn't leave the wards they were in; food and drinks were brought onto the wards on trolleys, so people did not need to go to a dining room.

I found it strange that no-one ever asked when they would be going home, and the sense of resignation was overwhelming. Perhaps it was never talked about as people never expected to have the chance to leave; they had become used to the idea that this was what life had to offer them.

A sad situation

What fascinated me so much was how the patients had organised themselves very well and created their own sub-culture within the ward, especially for the older people who had lived there for many years. The patients had established roles and positions within the hospital for themselves, usually completely informally and through their own recognition of other people's interests and skills. This determined who did the washing and who did the cleaning and tidying. Meanwhile, the ward sisters sat there in the office and did nothing and let it all happen.

When I was there, I felt a sense of sadness when looking through the patient notes as many of the people living at the hospital had been sent there during the 1920s by their own relatives and society. Other people at the hospital were there because they had a learning disability and people did not understand them.

I found a lot of the people working within the hospital did not provide the basic level of nursing input and I struggled to encourage them to understand and deliver good nursing practice which was respectful, professional and caring, with minimal success. The staff team showed no appreciation that they were running a small community of people and showed no sensitivity to people's roles or their sense of belonging within it, because they were the 'top dogs'.

During my time at Claybury Hospital, I observed patients being given the wrong teeth, everyone's teeth being brushed with the same brush also people with huge horrendous pressure sores with the staff having no clue about how to prevent or treat them.

I knew that if anyone began to behave in a troublesome way or started to require more attention, they then became too much bother and they would be medicated to subdue them. Drugs were freely available for the ward sister to access and she had the right to give these out as she saw fit. She wouldn't need to go via the doctor to get a prescription or go to a senior within the hospital to justify anything.

No-one to confide in

I was 21 and still very young at the time. None of my family members or friends had a similar job to the one I had at the hospital and this meant that I had no-one to confide in and talk to about what I was experiencing and observing. I didn't have a role model or family member to take counsel with.

At that time there was nothing out of the ordinary about having huge hospitals/institutions to house people who "didn't fit" into civil society. There was also nothing unusual about how Claybury Hospital was run as this is what was expected in these sorts of places. These types of hospitals were all over the place – thankfully that has changed, although institutional thinking still exists, and it can govern the way people are supported and treated by society.

When I now think about this place and I reflect on my time and experience there I still feel sad; it was a sad place and a place in which I would not be happy to have any family member or loved one of mine.

Through the community care movement of the 1990s and the initiative for people to be able to remain in their community and return to the community, Claybury Hospital was closed. There was a public inquiry held in 1997 and since the hospital's closure the building has been converted into luxury apartments.

Before we met – Peter's defining moment

Before I met my wonderful future husband, he was facing his own experiences.

Holly remembers Peter as clever, faithful and constant. There was sadness about him, a disappointment in the ways of humanity, but he had a great capacity for love and kindness, and truth.

Peter was born in Darjeeling India, nestled in the foothills of the Himalayas. Holly, Peter's twin sister, was born 10 minutes before Peter where his father was a Civil Engineer, building bridges and roads.

Whilst their upbringing was hardly traditional there bond was undeniable.

After the breakup of his parents' marriage, Peter and his twin were separated.

From their interlacing of their souls, twins walk side by side, both a shadow and a frame. Over their lives, even if they were apart for many years, time and place would slip away when Holly and Peter were together. They had a way of looking at one another, a quiet silence that never needed words.

Peter's mother brought his twin Holly back to England first. Peter later came home by boat with his Dad, who needed to avoid the bloodshed accompanying the partition of India.

Peter was sent to boarding school with a cruel headmaster, who in the coldest of winters, made the boys have a cold bath every morning!

When Peter's dad realised how unhappy his son was there he placed him at St Lawrence college in Kent, where Peter was very happy.

A defining moment happened for Peter which was very significant for him when he was at St Lawrence School. At about 12 years old, his scripture master had to leave the class and left them with some work too. They had to read a passage from the book of Isaiah chapter 16. This tells of a wonderful vision of the Lord ``high & lifted up''. In this passage the Lord askes "who shall I send and who will go for us? Peter answered in his own heart "Hear I am – send me". This was a significant memory in Peter's heart. This commitment was the direction for his life.

In 1959 Peter received his call up papers for his national service. Peter was a "conscientious objector" and because of this he refused to sign up. He had to go before a judge and tribunal to make sure he was genuine and authentic and not just trying to avoid the frontline.

A "conscientious objector" is a person who objects to war in any form and their objection must be sincere. A conscientious objector can claim the right to refuse to perform military service on the grounds of freedom of thought, conscience, and/or religion. Conscientious objectors are often assigned to an alternative civilian service as a substitute.

The judge and tribunal were very impressed with Peter and concluded that he was a genuine conscientious objector and they requested that he work at an old people's hospital as a porter for two years national service.

It was there where he met Phillip, a porter who took Peter under his wing, and they became very good friends. Peter loved the patients and he loved being at the hospital. Whilst on night duty all sorts of things happened which would keep him busy and occupied.

Peter recalls an occasion, while on night duty, when he and Phillip helped one of the doctors to restore his car; they took his car inside and stripped it down completely and put it right before morning.

These porters were also favoured by the cooks and the chief chef once looked in the fridge and said, "I have never seen so many legless chickens in my life!"

Meeting Peter

Whilst training to be a nurse I got to hear of a Christian community on Bradwell on Sea, called the Othona Community, which ran a summer camp. It was extremely cheap and a very welcome break for shattered nurses.

In 1961, after I had visited the summer camp a number of times, I went as an assistant cook to cater for 100 people and, whilst there, I met Peter.

We were both in our early 20s and I really fell for him, but he was oblivious of me!

I returned to Othona when I could, and I always looked forward to going as I loved the sixth century chapel where we worshipped. I loved the wild marshes and the seabirds over the pebbled shore, and I loved the company and the freedom.

There were bird watchers around and they showed us the plovers' nest – a little indentation with eggs that looked identical to the stones around them. There were mud flats with lovely warm soft mud and baby crabs scattering in and out and the creeks would fill up at high tide. On the land side of the sea wall were marshes with reed warblers, willow warblers and marsh buntings. When you sat on top of the sea wall, all you could hear were the wind, the rushes and birds. I loved it.

Our accommodation was in Nissen huts, prefabricated steel structures made from a half-cylindrical skin of corrugated steel. Originally designed during the First World War as temporary accommodation, they were very basic. The huts had 15-20 beds in each. Tents were also available, providing the option to camp. Whilst I spent time there I both camped in a tent and stayed in the huts. Across the bridge, well away from the camp, is where the chemical toilets were – they are best not mentioned!

We had to be self-sufficient at Othona; this included fetching drinking water in big tanks on wheels. It was a five-minute walk to get the tanks to the campsite after pulling them across the sand dunes!

The cost to go to the Othona summer camp was minimal and it was even better for a nurse as we received a nurse's discount. It was only £2 a week! The organiser, Norman Motley, had a soft spot for nurses and was very supportive of any nurse who wanted to attend the summer camp. I went whenever I could, for a couple of nights or for a week. I would fit my stays around my other commitments, which included work, family and church.

The memory of meeting Peter stayed with me and I did think about him, although he had forgotten me; I hadn't registered on his screen. So, every time I went to the Othona Community I hoped that I would see Peter again.

I went to Othona by myself and over time I got to know a number of people. I was confident that I would not feel alone; there would always be someone to spend time with whilst there.

Good friendships

I had struck up some good friendships at Othona, especially with Janet Motley, the organiser's daughter. I also became firm friends with Norrie, the chief cook, an Australian lady who you didn't argue and with a little boy of about 10 years old who popped in from time to time called Leemy Coupland. His dad had "brainstorms" so Leemy got out of the house and explored the country whenever he could. There was also Ruby, who was a character, but a sad, anxious and under-confident girl from Poplar (which is the place where *"Call the Midwife"* is filmed). She was often in distress and needed a lot of reassurance.

I continued to go to Othona as often as possible hoping that one day Peter, the young man who had so impressed me, would revisit and return. Then one day he did return! I was so thrilled. For him it was love at first sight. For me? Wow!! This gorgeous 'drop dead' handsome man had fallen in love with me! With me! Wow!

Being and falling in love is one of the most lasting and memorable experiences of my life. The memory of it has carried me through the many subsequent trials, stresses, problems and difficulties. Falling in love is well waiting for – even if you have to wait until you are 58 years old! Never settle for second best.

Promises of God

Faithful is He that calleth you, who also will perform it.

Peter was more than everything I had been hoping for.

People's reactions were mixed, at the time we were 21 and 23 years old.

He asked and I said yes

Peter proposed to me soon after our second meeting. He said he couldn't stand the tension of the long drive at weekends between Liverpool, where he was working at the time, and Essex, where I was based. He wanted us to be able to be together without the need for such a long drive. Peter proposed to me while we were sat in his car, a little Morris Minor called Tracy. I was delighted, and I was in love!

Peter was God's gracious, precious gift to me. I had prayed for a Christian husband and Peter was an answer to my prayers. He was tall, dark and handsome. A real gentleman, he was kind, gracious and very courteous. He was a lovely man, attentive, warm, and loving; and he was passionate for the Lord Jesus Christ.

At this time Peter was still in training as a paid apprentice with British Insulated Calendar's Cables and I was continuing with my career as a nurse.

I was not sure how my family were going to react to the news of the engagement, but I did know that they were not overly keen on Peter. In fact, one day, before Peter proposed, I was working in an orchard and my mum and dad were visiting the apple farm where I was helping with the harvest. They knew that Peter was going to arrive that day to see me and my Dad said: *'You are not going to see that young man again, are you? He is so arrogant.'* I knew then that my Dad was not keen, but my love for Peter was great and I knew I only wanted to be with him.

No!

After proposing to me, of course, Peter asked my dad for his blessing. My dad responded quite clearly *'NO!'* The question was such a shock to my dad, and he had been taken by surprise.

My dad wanted to hold onto his daughters, and he didn't want life to change; he wasn't ready to let go.

My mum spoke to Dad at length. She said: *'go on, let them'* and eventually she talked him around and he agreed to our engagement. My dad giving his approval meant everything to me and at that time in the 1960s it was important.

There was a mixture of shock, opposition, surprise and support for our marriage all around us, but we knew we were doing the right thing. Peter's Uncle Bob was supportive, *'You are good friends and that is what is important,'* he said, and the rest of Peter's family rallied together well and supported our relationship, engagement and future wedding.

My mum, sisters and eventually my dad were supportive of our engagement (even though Dad had agreed to it he still wasn't enthusiastic). However, my sister was a big tease, and would say things like, *'It must be because you're going to have ginger twins, that is why you are getting married so fast.'* I would find this annoying sometimes even though I knew this was her sense of humour, and she was just having a bit of fun.

A sad loss

Sadly, Peter's stepmother passed away before our wedding. We were all upset about this. She had been very kind, understanding and sweet to Peter and his twin sister Holly.

Peter often regretted his treatment of his stepmother; his younger years had been very difficult and turbulent for Peter and he often took his unhappiness and frustration out on his stepmother. He was very young when his mum had left his dad, him and his sister behind, and this had left him feeling neglected and unloved, which scarred his view of family.

Later in life Peter realised that all the negative and destructive thoughts and words which his mother shared following the separation and subsequent divorce were to justify her actions when leaving his dad. His mum's thoughts and words were not a reflection on the character of his dad, whose behaviour had been pretty good, but his mum's words had caused him a great deal of confusion, distress and mixed emotions.

Peter had been greatly influenced by his mother's poison. She would often say very negative and mean things that would affect his opinions of his stepmother. It was hard for Peter to know what to think when the two people who mattered most in his life were telling him such contrasting things and treating him in such different ways. Peter found all this too traumatic to deal with and thus he wanted nothing to do with families.

I wonder if Peter ever fully recovered from this.

Moving to Liverpool

The winter before our wedding was very cold. I went to care for Peter's landlady, in Liverpool. She was dying from renal failure and I nursed her whilst I was there. Peter and I did not live together in the same house, although we both lived in Liverpool. The landlady's son still lived at the house, and it was very difficult for him. His mum being ill and a stranger in the house taking care of her was a hard situation to be in.

I remember trying to keep her warm, and he refused to let me heat the house. Sometimes I did heat the house without his say-so and he would then open the loft door and let all the heat out. He would say that he was worried that the attic tank would freeze over, which didn't make a great deal of sense and at the time his mum's comfort was my priority. I found him very difficult to be around but continued to try my best to ease his mum's pain and to comfort her. It must have been a very stressful time for him.

Here comes the bride

Peter and I married the following March, in 1963, much to the dismay of our families – they thought that it was far too quick. I know they would have all preferred it if we had continued to have a lengthy engagement, perhaps for a few years before taking the step of marriage, as this is what they would have done, but we knew what we wanted.

After the wedding we started making plans for our future.

We were going to have six children, most of them adopted because we recognised that there were many children that needed a good home.

Peter had also wanted to be a missionary but at the time we met, Peter was in a fantastic job and he had it absolutely made. When I asked him if he had any ambition he said *'no, I have reached the top'* – it was a good place to reach at such a young age. He said: *'when you work in a very big company you do not have ambitions like that, maybe an ambition to be a senior officer but I have become one anyway.'*

My aspiration was to be the very best I could be for Peter, to give him all my love.

Quick flit

After our wedding we first lived in a small flat in a friend's house. We loved our first place. We had a kitchen and one large room with a bed, table, armchair and carpet, and we shared the bathroom with our friends. On talking to Peter's Uncle Bob about our belongings he said, *'do not worry about only having one armchair, you only need one armchair when you are first married.'* The flat was in Liverpool and, after we had been there a short while, it became clear that these friends where not as nice as we had been first led to believe.

We decided to do a "quick flit" to a prefab which we had been told about and we shared this with Mr Frost. Phillip, who worked with Peter at the hospital, was his son-in-law, and we got on just fine.

The prefab was a prefabricated house. They were legally outlined in 1944 by Winston Churchill as a response to the housing stock shortage after the devastation of the Second World War. They were intended to be temporary accommodation to last up to 10 years, but people still live in them today.

It was lovely, always sunny, small, cosy and well-equipped. We crammed all our furniture in with Mr Frost's, including the furniture that family had given us and the things we had saved money for and bought.

We did not have a lot of room! We had our own bedroom, but we shared all the other rooms with Mr Frost, but he was usually out as he spent a lot of time over the road at his daughter's house.

Phillip, the hospital porter, and his wife Eva lived over the path in their prefab with their two boys, Ernest and Keith. Once Peter was explaining to Keith how he used to do something, and Keith replied, *'yes but that was in the olden days.'* (!)

Although we were very happy living in Liverpool and sharing with Mr Frost, Peter was becoming increasingly concerned for his dad as he was on his own and widowed. Peter felt he ought to be close to him to be able to support him.

Moving to Essex

We spoke at length about moving to Essex and we decided we should move to Saffron Walden to be closer to Peter's dad.

In 1963 we took the leap and we moved from Liverpool to Essex into Peter's dad's house. At the same time Peter started searching for a more satisfying job and he found a place to work that seemed to suit him well at Crittalls Windows in Braintree, Essex.

When Peter secured the job, we moved out of Peter's dad's house and into our own home close to Peter's place of employment. We found a lovely place to live – a tiny new house on a new estate which was just right for us. We were very friendly with our neighbours, Julie and Bob, and we entertained a lot in between shift work.

William Julian Courtauld Hospital

Whilst we lived in Braintree, I worked in the local cottage hospital, William Julian Courtauld Hospital (which no longer exists). This cottage hospital catered for the entire district. At the hospital there was a long corridor and at one end of the corridor was an operating theatre, the men's ward and a large casualty room. In this casualty room a nurse could be left alone to manage all the casualties coming in from all over the district.

The casualty ward also had a morning hand clinic for hand injuries. I was often the staff nurse in charge of the entire hospital in the evening. I was left in charge of everything; I had to handle absolutely anything that might come in. I am very glad that I didn't have to handle the situation in which a child had been crushed by a wardrobe!

Moving along the corridor there was the front door, kitchens and the staff dining room and to the other end were several side wards and two larger women's wards.

The cleaner there was a lovely young lady called Aliyah, full of smiles and kindness. She had a learning disability herself and she was under threat of having her child taken away from her because of this. In those days for people deemed as being "incapable" of taking care of their own child this was the norm. Aliyah and her boyfriend were in love, so just wanted to make love together. The cook at the hospital firmly told them this was *sinful and wicked.'* Although I never knew what happened to Aliyah, I do hope she has had a happy life.

Hot chocolate sauce

The dining room at William Julian Courtauld Hospital was small, cosy, and lined with armchairs. The cook made whatever we wanted, and the doctors and other hospital staff would sit together to eat, a group of 12 or more with the Matron at the head of the table. I enjoyed being part of this team; they were a friendly and hardworking bunch. It was a good atmosphere, with a wonderful group of people and being able to spend time together like this was very enlightening. (My favourite William Julian Courtauld kitchen memory is of huge jugs of hot chocolate sauce and innumerable 'briquettes' of vanilla ice cream.)

We knew the whole district and they all knew us; at that time Braintree was a small country town, not the sprawling place it is now, and we played a really important role in that community.

Rescue

On one occasion at the hospital the outhouses and sheds were turned out to find items for an upcoming bonfire. Nige Gosling was about to light the wood that had been stacked, when Peter noticed that he was going to burn a dilapidated old wheel-backed chair (this would have been quite a purchase when bought for new and was built to the highest quality using the finest craftsmanship and wood). Peter rescued it and renovated it back to its former glory. We still have this chair at home; it is beautiful. We also rescued a huge oval fish kettle made of thick aluminium from an outhouse for jams and preserves, this was very useful.

Starting a family

During this period of our lives Peter and I had friends around us. We cooked and entertained a lot and talked until the small hours. Everything was great, and we were enjoying life. We had wanted to start a family and we were ready. So, we started to plan and make arrangements. My mum hoped that we would have a child that would be born on the same day as her birthday.

We had been trying for our first child and after a short period of time I was pregnant. We were delighted. I was showing all the signs of being pregnant. In those days, we didn't have pregnancy tests. Instead you would wait until your body started to change; a missed period and beginning to feel sick are both indicators that you may be pregnant. At this stage you would go to see your doctor. So that is what we did, and the doctor confirmed that I was pregnant. We were both delighted on hearing the news of the pregnancy; our wishes were coming true.

All sorts of things start to go through your mind when you are expecting a child; you think about timing (when is our baby going to arrive? Will we be ready? Do we have everything we need?) and baby clothes and wonder if the house will be ready for a baby. I wanted to feel ready in every way and I wanted to learn how to be ready to be a mum. I started to read a book I had come across called "Natural Childbirth". I found that this was very interesting and informative and easy to follow. I did not feel overwhelmed by what I read, and it was not at all complicated like it is today.

We were surrounded by many kind and loving country folk. My colleagues, patients, friends and the local people we knew were so generous. I was given 42 hand knitted matinee sets, bonnets and coats with gloves and booties – that's a lot! We had all the clothes for our new baby that we could possibly need. We were very pleased; we received many kind gifts.

Although we had received a lot of generous gifts, there were still some items that we needed. So, we decided to buy everything else we needed second-hand and, after some searching, we managed to acquire a cot, pushchair, pram, baby bouncers, play pen, blankets, everything we needed before Simon arrived. We finally felt ready and set for our wonderful baby to arrive and to start family life.

Peter's job

Whilst I was pregnant and expecting our first child it became apparent that the job that Peter had taken was proving to be unsatisfactory; Peter felt that it wasn't utilising all his skills. They had employed him specifically for his skillset and experience as the company had made a commitment to embrace new technologies and approaches that Peter was well versed in, but this was not happening.

Peter decided to stick it out a bit longer and in doing so he had the opportunity to attend a number of valuable training courses offered by the company, which added to his skills. Whilst training, he found some useful contacts at a company called MTM Consultants. This included Gerome Lumb, who was a consultant at MTM. They developed a strong friendship, and this is the one person Peter has kept in touch with over the years.

Peter continued to take part in more training, but he continued to be dissatisfied with his current employment.

Outside work our relationship continued to be enjoyable and we were still strong, happy and very much looking forward to welcoming our first child into the world and caring for them.

A sudden change of plan

In September 1965 Simon was born in the maternity unit at William Julian Courtauld, the local cottage hospital where I had worked before becoming pregnant.

Peter's friend Gerome from MTM Consultants was with us on the night I went into labour. We had made plans to go and see *Mary Poppins* at the cinema and we were all getting ready to go when our plans had to quickly change.

As I was taken to hospital to give birth to our first child, they continued to the cinema!

Full of excitement and nerves

After Simon was born, they kept me in hospital for a longer period than I expected and at the time I was not sure what the reason was. I was starting to feel concerned that they had found something unusual about my baby and wanted to check him out – but they were keeping me in the dark.

I realised that most women only stayed in for a few days after childbirth, but I ended up being there for a fortnight.

During my stay in hospital there were some mums on the same ward. These were local girls who were married to the American servicemen based at Weathersfield airbase and serving within the Vietnam War. These women came to have their babies and would only stay a few days before they went home, which emphasised to me how unusual it was for me to still be there. The American ladies were also expected to go back to America when their husbands returned from the conflict in Vietnam, no matter how soon after childbirth.

New life new mum

After giving birth I was very tired. I could see other mums coming, giving birth and going home, which concerned me, but there was also a part of me that was thankful as I knew I needed the rest. I was exhausted.

During my stay at the hospital Peter would write to me every day. He would send me a letter first thing in the morning, and I would receive it the same day! How times have changed! In 1965 there were two posts a day!

Returning home

When I was discharged from hospital and I returned home, I was still very exhausted. Peter was a great help and he did a lot for Simon and me and around our home. After six weeks I had recuperated and had enough energy to go out. At this point I realised and appreciated how fantastic Peter was with our new baby, Simon. He was attentive, calm, reassuring and comforting and he had a real gift of "baby loving" and baby talk.

First trip out

We lived 10 minutes' walk from Braintree town centre, which didn't seem far for me when I was fit and healthy but after so much time of rest it was daunting. I needed to get to the shops for items that we needed so I had a goal, and this gave me the motivation to get there. Although it was a real challenge, I did it… onwards and upwards. From there, nothing was going to hold me back.

Entertaining

I always imagined that the entertaining and socialising we had done before Simon had arrived in our lives would continue into our future. We had done this so regularly and had a tight circle of friends. Although we tried, this did start to change after Simon arrived in our lives. I appreciate now that this is the case for all couples when they start a family.

We were tired from sleepless nights and Simon's routine became our routine.

As Simon's condition became more apparent and we began to realise it, along with everyone else in our lives, a separation began to happen between ourselves and close family and friends – a mutual distancing.

Family life

Later on, we moved to a second house in Braintree. We had a nice garden. It had a long front garden with trees down one side of the drive and a willow tree at the bottom; this grew well there as it was very damp. Peter was a good gardener and he enjoyed planning projects for the garden. We had settled in Braintree and we had made some good friendships with our neighbours.

We often helped out with the gardening for friends who lived close by, especially when they went on holiday. Once we were asked if we would water their vegetables and we were invited to take what we would like to eat. So, we had access to freshly harvested vegetables. On one occasion I took some of their handsome cauliflowers, but they were so full of caterpillars and other creepy crawlies that they must have been more animal than vegetable! It was dreadful trying to wash them all out!

While we lived in Braintree, although we continued to be Christians with a strong faith, we didn't go to church as we had not found a place where we wanted to worship in the area.

A handy dad

While we lived in Braintree my Dad was very handy and he helped Peter floor the loft with some waste doors. Simon was less than one year old then and my Dad gave up smoking for Simon's healing. Until this point, he had been a smoker all his life and he gave it up fast. My Dad prayed every night and I am sure that he included Simon in these prayers. As my story unfolds there was a long period of no contact between me and my family. This was a huge separation, but at a later time after we had reconciled, I found out that Simon remained in Dad's prayers throughout – this was his way, I imagine, of coping and still having a connection to us.

Searching for baptism

In latter parts of 1964 whilst I was pregnant with Simon, Peter started to long for the Baptism of the Holy Spirit, and he went to Liverpool for this ministry. We realised that we had to find a place with a lively Christian fellowship.

People's reaction to cri du chat

Simon was still a young baby and we had started to take him out in the pram. In those days it was normal to park a baby's pram outside the shop, leave the baby inside the pram and go inside to join the queue, and this is what I used to do. It was whilst queuing in a shop that I first noticed the reaction of strangers to my baby. Simon had a different cry, unusual, like a cat crying – it was very strange to passers-by and to the other customers. I would overhear their comments: *'What is that noise?' 'Have you heard that baby or is that a cat?'*

Simon was later diagnosed with a condition called cri du chat or 5p minus syndrome. This is a genetic condition present from birth, which has a range of symptoms. One such symptom is one that affects the vocal cords, creating problems with speech.

To see me through

We had no other way than the way forward and we could see no alternative other than to take it to the Lord in prayer. We had the knowledge that we were right to believe in Simon. We read some good books by Christian authors that turned out to be very helpful books. I also sang a lot of hymns and kept a hymn book in the kitchen.

God is my refuge and strength, a very present help in trouble.

I wrote out many strengthening scripture posters and stuck them on the walls.

The gas board

In 1965 when Simon was very young, Peter secured a job as an engineer at the gas board in Shipley, Bradford.

This job enabled Peter to use the skills he had acquired during the recent courses he had attended, and he was looking forward to putting these skills into practice.

Whilst at the interview for the gas board, Peter talked about his training and was employed to stop a threatened strike. The approach Peter took ensured the workers were paid a bonus scheme as a reward for working well. It stopped the strike and brought about a good feeling between the workers and manager. He was popular with the workers as he improved their working conditions, and with the managers as the workforce became committed, reliable and efficient.

Peter was brilliant at his job. He was a work study engineer and people were very glad to have him around. A work study engineer studies how people function within the workplace and identifies ways to improve working practices and increase efficiencies, which includes making it easier for the worker.

Moving 'up north'

After securing the job, Peter made contact with an old friend, Emily, who lived in Bradford. Whilst Simon and I remained in Braintree, Peter moved up to Shipley to start his new job and he rented a room with Emily and her mother.

Emily was a kind and lovely Christian lady. She was an elder at her church and she had known very hard times as a child. She had a misshapen foot as a paving stone had fallen on it as a child, and at the time her family could not afford a doctor to take care of her and her broken foot and provide the treatment that she needed.

They lived in a small back-to-back house; their little garden was the size of a pocket handkerchief, but the prettiest I have ever seen.

Mission: find a home!

Peter and Emily set about looking for a house for us to move into as a family. They found a lovely property, a new Wimpey house at the top of a hill on a new estate overlooking Bradford, in Allerton. We left our house in Braintree in November 1966. We were sorry to leave our life in Braintree, our home and our neighbours, but this was a new life for us, new beginnings and we were looking forward to the adventure of it all. We moved into our brand-new house on the Allerton estate when Simon was one year old.

60 mill chimneys

At that time, you could see 60 mill chimneys from the hillside at Allerton.

We liked our new home, the garden and the views. It was also close to a fellowship we had found and started to attend called "The New Covenant Fellowship".

We were pleased to be involved with the New Covenant Fellowship, who took us to their hearts. They especially showed this through their hospitality; we would go to see people and have meals with them. We would in turn invite them to our new home to enjoy a meal. It felt like we belonged, and we had a strong network of friends.

Holy Ghost

During this time Peter contacted his old friend, Norman, who was now a curate. Harry immediately and urgently referred Peter to a Christian conference centre in the Wirral where they were experiencing outstanding spiritual experiences. Peter visited and whilst there he was immediately baptised in the Holy Ghost. This was the start of some big changes for Peter; he gave up smoking at the age of 26.

Loving our new home

We loved our new home in Allerton, Bradford, and wanted to make it ours.

We soon made plans for our big new garden. Before we moved there, it was a fenceless waste of weeds; we had to get the weeds under control and add a garden fence to provide us with some privacy and a safe place for Simon to play in. Peter was a keen gardener and we spent a lot of time planning it and working on it. I'm delighted to say it became a gorgeous garden which we enjoyed, and we were very pleased with it.

We purchased what we needed from the beautifully illustrated *"Bees"* catalogue and it was lovingly worked.

We spent a lot on the garden. We planted three fruit trees along the bottom of the garden; there was a Queen Elizabeth rose hedge at the back and we also had a bed of wild strawberries, gooseberries and blackcurrants. There was a weeping cherry tree and a weeping willow. We enjoyed having a chamomile and lavender rockery; it all smelt lovely and it was pleasing to the eye. We also planned for this to be a fun place for Simon and we added a sandpit for him to play in.

We created a gorgeous outdoor space which eased all the senses.

For us, the garden was a source of calm and tranquillity and a delight to have.

Revisiting the past

In 2010 I re-visited this first home in Bradford, just to have a look. Our beautiful garden had gone altogether; the present owner had replanted it and it looked very nice and quite different to the garden we had created. The new owners said that the house had had a very difficult history and that they had bought it in a bad state.

Oppression

Living at Allerton had started well and full of promise but over a short period of time the cracks began to show and life in Allerton was not turning out as well as we hoped. We soon started to feel that this area of delight, our garden, was really oppressed by the neighbours. There were people shouting and screaming, especially children, all day and all night. It happened more so because our home was on a corner and both our next door neighbours visited each other by crossing over our garden, which became a huge source of frustration.

This was the first time we had lived on a new estate and we began to question whether this is what happened on a new estate like this.

We knew then that we didn't like living on a new estate in this position and if we were to move again, we would choose a different type of home, an established one in an established area with an established community.

Someone even stole fruit from our trees!

All the things that were taking place around us in the neighbourhood were things that Simon couldn't do or take part in. He couldn't go out and join in the games that were being played on the street. He didn't have the understanding to know how to play the games and the other children would ignore and avoid him or – worse still – tease him and stare.

As for ourselves being accepted as part of that community, Peter and I didn't necessarily want to spend all day gossiping on the street. We didn't enjoy talking about other people's business or being negative about others. We were interested in music, serious subjects and loving Jesus and society. We preferred those topics of conversation. We felt that we were living somewhere that we didn't belong.

All the people living on the estate were new to the area and they had moved away from everything they had known. In this new place they didn't know how to behave with each other or how to respond to each other's likes and dislikes.

In established communities, people are better placed to know how to avoid over familiarity as relationships have been established over a long period of time; the social norms have been long established and understood.

In this new place chaos seemed to rule. In this estate we weren't happy about how people behaved or how they parented their children.

We felt isolated and not a part of the world around us.

Unease

Back then I began to realise that, although the estate was full of new babies, and babies on the way, we – Simon and I – were bad news for the other mothers and babies.

People avoided us; we were not included in social gatherings. This was very blatant as we could see neighbours and their children visiting others' houses on the estate for social events. This would happen on a regular basis and we were simply not invited. Everyone had moved to the estate at a similar time, late 1965, so everyone had an equal amount of time to form friendships and I had made efforts to get to know people. I offered to cook,

I chatted in passing, I offered to help others, but these efforts were largely ignored. I felt embarrassed, sad and lonely at times. Our neighbours made it really clear that they didn't want us around much and it was uncomfortable. I tried to understand the situation that we found ourselves in and decided that it was unkind to get too involved with other people, as we were clearly an object of fear. I could find no other answer to rationalise what we were experiencing. There was never a particular situation where this was clearly stated by any of the young mums, but I noticed their reactions. Coming to this conclusion also reflected how I was feeling.

I couldn't share in their discussions and chats about family life – the sorrows and joys – as we were stuck in a completely different experience of starting a family. The other mothers would not understand if I tried to share with them what was happening in our family and what we were learning about Simon. How could they understand? They had no insight into what our life was like. I was scared to tell them as I didn't want my family to be even more ostracised. Anyway, I hardly knew how to express it. How do you put it into words?

We were living life with a difference – a disability, but at this stage nothing had been recognised, diagnosed or explained. We were just different and because of this we didn't relate well to others. Here's how it was.

This little story that was shared with me in 2008 sums it all up.

Welcome to Holland

'I am often asked to describe the experience of raising a child with a disability – to try to help people who have not shared that unique experience to understand it, to imagine how it would feel. It's like this......

Welcome To Holland by Emily Perl Kingsley

I am often asked to describe the experience of raising a child with a disability - to try to help people

who have not shared that unique experience to understand it, to imagine how it would feel. It's like this......

When you're going to have a baby, it's like planning a fabulous vacation trip - to Italy. You buy a bunch

of guide books and make your wonderful plans. The Coliseum. The Michelangelo David. The gondolas in

Venice. You may learn some handy phrases in Italian. It's all very exciting.

After months of eager anticipation, the day finally arrives. You pack your bags and off you go. Several

hours later, the plane lands. The flight attendant comes in and says, "Welcome to Holland."

"Holland?!?" you say. "What do you mean Holland?? I signed up for Italy! I'm supposed to be in Italy.

All my life I've dreamed of going to Italy."

But there's been a change in the flight plan. They've landed in Holland and there you must stay.

The important thing is that they haven't taken you to a horrible, disgusting, filthy place, full of

pestilence, famine and disease. It's just a different place.

So you must go out and buy new guide books. And you must learn a whole new language. And you will

meet a whole new group of people you would never have met.

It's just a different place. It's slower-paced than Italy, less flashy than Italy. But after you've been

there for a while and you catch your breath, you look around.... and you begin to notice that Holland has

windmills....and Holland has tulips. Holland even has Rembrandts.

But everyone you know is busy coming and going from Italy... and they're all bragging about what a

wonderful time they had there. And for the rest of your life, you will say "Yes, that's where I was

supposed to go. That's what I had planned."

And the pain of that will never, ever, ever, ever go away... because the loss of that dream is a very very

significant loss.

But... if you spend your life mourning the fact that you didn't get to Italy, you may never be free to

enjoy the very special, the very lovely things ... about Holland.

Appreciation

When you are going through difficult times emotionally and financially, it really makes you appreciate what you have in life. The small things that people may take for granted suddenly become significant and hugely important. For instance, I have a handwritten recipe book in which I started to collect recipes in 1965, a time when we were very poor and homeless. I have treasured this and still use it today. The book is a selection of recipe contributions from many people who I have met along the way. It meant so much to me that people were prepared to offer their help in any way they could, and this included sharing recipes for good food when living on a tight budget. People shared family recipes that had been passed down generations and this meant so much to me.

Downward spiral

After a year of our new life in Bradford we also began to feel criticism from members of The New Covenant Fellowship, a place where we originally had felt a great sense of welcome and acceptance.

We felt a change of "temperature" there. Our trusted friend informed us that members of the Fellowship had been told by the lady in charge to no longer visit and see us and to stay away.

We were never given an explanation and we began to believe that we were seen as a problem as we were deemed as being unhealed, due to Simon's condition. Peter had also been told that he had the "wrong attitude". The lady in charge would have thought that we were "in sin" as our circumstances with Simon indicated that we had sinned and, as he was not responding well to their attempts at "healing", this opinion was strengthened further. As we had made it clear that we did not welcome the attempt to "heal" Simon because we accepted and loved him as he was and did not believe he needed "fixing" or "healing", everything was therefore entirely our fault.

Peter did not have a bad attitude, but he did question the practices in the Fellowship, and he did not always do things the way the rest of the Fellowship did things. At that time, I was not able to comprehend that he had mental health problems.

Changing perceptions

Peter was brilliant at his job at the gas board and he was working very hard under intense pressure. He always delivered the goods, but he came to the firm belief that his immediate boss was evil and "against him".

There was no absolute evidence that he was being treated unfairly, but Peter's perceptions of his situation began to change, and the stress of his role began to take its toll and tip him.

I just believed that everything he did was right and everyone else was wrong; the possibility that he could have a mental health problem did not enter my head, in fact this possibility of a mental health problem did not enter my head for 30 years, so we just had to swim against the tide and face adverse reactions.

He was my husband and I wanted to support him and have trust in him. Things were not helped by the current thinking in our church which was for wives to be 'subject' to their husbands.

It's not until much later in my life I look back and see that rather than agreeing with Peter whilst his mood was changing, I maybe should have encouraged him to think positively and counteract his negative feelings and thoughts, which is what I do now.

Leaving the gas board

Peter's work and his whole situation became too difficult for him and he left the gas board in 1970, when we had been in Bradford for four years. He was 32 years old and he would never seek further employment after this stage in his life.

Peter's negative perceptions were not purely work related and they began to extend to our home life as he felt that all the neighbours were victimising us. Without an income or any close friendships, we began to feel and become increasingly isolated.

Purging from the past

The negativity escalated further, and Peter decided that we must purge ourselves of all the links with the past. Peter was obsessed and insistent that we remove any connection with the past. There was no time to think about it or to consider the consequences. I went along with what Peter wanted; I loved him, respected him and unequivocally trusted that he knew best. I never stopped once to question him or his actions.

Breaking these links involved not contacting people. We could not respond to anyone, friends or family, or to Peter's side of the family or my side of the family's attempts to contact us. Peter insisted on clearing out any objects and items that linked us to any person from our past: Wedding presents! Engagement presents! Personal gifts! Beautiful necklaces! Precious craft boxes! Exquisite wine glasses! This was a huge and very negative turning point in our lives. This was a very sad time that devastated our families and caused scars that would never heal. We lost so much time with those who loved us most and would have done anything to protect us.

However, the bin men had a ball. They were thrilled when they came to us, sifting through our treasures ready to take to their own home!

Distancing from my parents

During this purge when my family did try to contact me, I would be very curt with them. I used to blame this on my dad, who would phone up and be very angry and complaining. I was loved by them in their way, but they didn't understand what I was going through or why I was cutting them out of my life and eventually I reached the stage where I didn't understand them; their life was so different to what mine had become.

Breaking ties

On one dreadful occasion my parents came up from the south by car with gifts. They had travelled a long distance and braved some bad fog to make the journey.

At the time they were in their 50s and this was a huge trek for them both.

Due to this newfound resolve which I had unquestioningly supported Peter in, I didn't even open the door to them. I left them stood on the doorstep confused, upset, angry and neglected. They had no idea about Peter leaving his job, his changing moods and his deep desire to purge us of our past ties and links.

I say this now with sorrow. After this we were out of contact with them for two years and after that we went 30 years without seeing each other.

In those 32 years I did not answer communications with my parents even though they tried so hard and they never gave up. They would travel all the way and park outside our house and gaze at the windows in the hope of catching a glimpse of us. They would also write letters to us on occasions, birthdays and at Christmas but we never replied.

They tried to ring at first but stopped after they were not successful; we simply would not answer the phone and eventually it stopped ringing.

Through all this they never received an explanation, just a silence.

I think I was always on my parents' mind and this must have caused a lot of pain for them – I was their first baby.

So many adolescents want to leave home as they can no longer relate to their parents; how different this could be with some mutual compassion and consideration. My situation as an adult could have been so different with some mutual openness, understanding and patience too.

Isn't this what happens to people when they join a cult?! I was led, controlled and brainwashed by the man I had married, and I went along with it hook, line and sinker.

Increased isolation

At this time, we were completely isolated; we had cut ties with neighbours, friends and family.

Some people had decided to stay away from us or to distance themselves, but largely the isolation we experienced was brought on by ourselves. We had become suspicious of everyone, their intentions and their opinions of us as a family.

This situation made us defensive and, in turn, we became judgemental of others and regarded ourselves as holier than everyone else.

Bad attitudes

All these feelings of disconnection started to spiral out of control, and our own attitudes towards others began to change for the worse. The feelings we had for others started to be reflected in how we treated the people around us; we were so suspicious of everybody.

This had been initially caused by the stress Peter experienced at work and the bad feelings this caused, which were later fuelled by the lack of support from "friends" at the church. No support was forthcoming as the people in the congregation didn't know how to respond to Peter and the paranoid thoughts he was experiencing. They handled him very badly and this led to Peter's wellbeing and outlook on life getting much worse.

This negatively influenced me, and I forgot or did not keep any of the laws of hospitality myself, which I had followed so graciously in previous years. On one occasion, when it had been snowing, our very nice post woman slipped in the snow. I am very ashamed to say this, but when she knocked on the door and stood there with blood all over her face, I did not invite her in to offer her any care, or to give her some rest or time to warm and recuperate. I only offered her something to wipe her face with but then sent her on her way. How terrible that was! I was just so consumed with suspicions about other people's motives and afraid of them too. I am so ashamed when I think back.

There was a lot of unkindness and misunderstanding surrounding me at that time, but I can clearly remember one lady who was kind and I remember her well – Mrs Jacobs. She lived over the road from us, and she was a breath of fresh air. She was always positively kind to us and purposely compassionate. She always made time to talk to us. She had six children herself, so she didn't have a lot of time. She was a good lady and we felt her goodness and kindness.

Unemployed

At the time when Peter became unemployed, we did not even consider accessing support from social services. Peter was afraid that if we did approach social services for support, they would get too involved in our lives and separate us as they became aware of our circumstances – especially Simon's circumstance – and Peter thought that they would turn him onto the street or, in his words, "into the hedges".

Devastation

Peter's dad was devastated when he learnt that Peter was unemployed; it was something he had never ever allowed to happen in his own life and his expectation was that Peter would hold the same value and principle.

We were living on no income; we were using our savings and we had to make them last. We had to adapt to a very different way of life very quickly.

Peter's dad began to provide a small allowance to help us get by. Praise God for Peter's dad.

Getting Resourceful

I used to make fantastic cardboard toys for Simon, by laminating layers of cardboard with glue. They were lovingly painted; bright and colourful with lots of variety and fun. The toys had to be strong to be "Simon proof" and withstand his enthusiasm. We made garages, mills, traction engines and cranes, which kept Simon entertained for hours.

For the little girl over the road, Angela, who was very sensible and kind, I made a doll's house. Angela loved her new toy and really appreciated having her very own doll's house.

Finding his voice

I had never heard Peter sing before but during this time I heard him sing for the first time. He would sing for hours with such a beautiful voice – like silk – that people would stand on their doorsteps to listen.

Visiting Devon

At this time Peter's sister, Holly, lived in Devon where she was the school nurse at a public school.

We could not afford a holiday and we were fortunate that Holly invited us to stay at her cottage so we could get away. We had a blissful month there in the summer in her old cottage called "The Coop". The walls were made of red Devon clay 15 feet deep – it was very snug.

Finances

Our financial situation was getting worse and in late 1971 our bank balance was £456 and steadily decreasing. We knew that very soon it would be £0. A sweet friend of ours called Carolyn gave us money when she could. We, in turn, later tried to support Carolyn financially through her studies at Bible College when we were in a better financial situation ourselves.

In March 1972 we received our rates bill for £100. This was a great deal of money and we had no money to pay the bill. We were desperate.

The final straw

We faced a brick wall. We had no ways or means of paying this bill. We decided we had to sell up and move on.

We believed that the Lord wanted us to go somewhere but we didn't know where. Fortunately, we sold the house quickly but where were we going to go? What were we even to do?

Homeless

The house was sold and all the belongings we could not part with or needed had been packed into our car, the rest was in storage and Simon was in the back of the car with basic necessities. We set off driving south.

Where to? We had no idea where we were going; we were simply hoping and expecting to receive direction from the Lord as to our destination, but also feeling rather desperate.

The first thing which seemed to confront us on our drive was a large advertising board, advertising funerals! This was not a good start to the journey.

We were homeless.

Where would we sleep at night?

Where would we find welcome?

Where would we live?

Where would we go next and how?

How would we protect and care for Simon?

That night we ended up in a hotel in the Midlands. We booked in and made a coffee in our room but before we even took a sip, we had spilt it over everything! We used all their towels to mop it up. It was terrifying!!

Police search

The hotel in the Midlands just didn't feel right, so we checked out, and headed on towards a trusted old friend of Peter's, who lived in Stafford. On the way down there was a motorway inspection and the police were inspecting every car; they seemed to be looking for someone.

We really panicked because as we had no fixed 'abode' we couldn't give them an address for where we lived or for where we were going.

The policeman shone his torch into our car and he called out to his mate: *'This one's okay Ted, the back is full of kids'*, which of course it wasn't, but that is what he saw!

Stafford

The friend in Stafford was less welcoming at having a family descend upon him unannounced in a tense and stressed out state.

He let us stay but we only stayed a few days.

We tried many other avenues, phone calls and leads and could find nowhere to go – it was desperate!

Parents

With no other options available to us we landed with my parents, with whom we had not been in contact for two years – my parents whose attempts at contacting us we had ignored and whom we had left on our doorstep when they had driven a great distance to attempt to visit us.

I found it impossible to communicate our situation to them. We couldn't really understand it ourselves, let alone express it. They were completely unable to comprehend it.

With the distress, paranoia, loss and isolation, the atmosphere was understandably tense. They put us up for one night but said we would have to go the next day as they were expecting a visitor, a minister.

There wasn't much love lost between Peter and my dad beforehand and now there was none.

Essex

We then went to stay with another old friend of Peter's in Essex, Philip Tates. By this time it was spring 1972 and we had only driven away from our home in Allerton two weeks prior.

This was an amazing experience. Philip had a lot of children – 12 or more – and the house was chaos and a tip, completely disorganised.

They were an unconventional family and I think this is why they were more sympathetic to our circumstances. We slept on a mattress on the floorboards and poor Simon just had a sleeping bag.

Whilst we stayed with Peter's friend, my father came to visit and brought some flowers. I think this may have been an apology for sending us away. This was comforting for me to know that my dad still cared.

We stayed a week with Philip Tates but during this time Peter's paranoia heightened and his mental health declined. He became increasingly convinced that Philip was also practising sorcery against us! Peter felt that we needed to escape and get away.

More anguish

When our position with the Tates family became untenable it became anguishing. We had tried all avenues and pushed many doors to find a place to stay and live.

After leaving the Tates' household we began a hard, long drive down to Exeter to go to a Christian Fellowship house we had discovered. This occupied several large terraced houses and we had heard that it was well run, well organised and kind. It was here that we started our "Fun Books", exercise books that we used for teaching Simon and illustrating everything we had seen.

When we arrived, we received a warm welcome – at last we had found somewhere to rest our weary heads and hearts.

They gave us a nice large room and in exchange we gave them £10 a week. I really enjoyed having our own room and we helped with all the housework and maintenance. Peter helped with all the odd jobs and handywork. We shared communal meals around a large table in the cellar room with other residents and many visiting guests. There were quite a few people living there and we had mid-week and Sunday prayer meetings.

We dedicated the afternoons to Simon, and we drove him out to give him opportunities to learn from all our surroundings.

We had been settled at the Christian Fellowship for four months when cracks began to appear. Peter started to feel judged and "got at" and he started to share his thoughts that the people there were narrow-minded.

At about this time I had dyed an old T-shirt of Peter's a bright colour and they felt this was a psychedelic colour and was "sinful!" Both myself and Peter felt judged for this.

The relationship between Peter and the organiser of the Fellowship began to deteriorate, and Peter increasingly felt that the Fellowship staffs were against us.

We started packing and thinking about where our next home would be.

Salterton

Our next home was with May, a friend who lived in Budleigh, Salterton. May hated cooking and loved gardening. In exchange for her generosity in providing us with a home, we did all the housekeeping, the cooking, shopping and we trimmed the grass and the hedge. We gave her £4 a week.

We arrived during a sunny autumn; we had lovely times visiting the nearby beaches strewn with cuttlebones, talking to local people, getting to know the fishermen and learning as much as we could about the sea and that environment.

The beaches around there are made of pebbles and when they are wet with seawater, they are very beautiful; some are actually semi-precious.

While we lived with May, we entertained people from our local Exeter Fellowship. American Air Force men were part of the Fellowship. This is when we met Ben from Texas. We went on to write to one another for a long time.

Although initially the arrangement with May had worked well, after a while, things became very tense. It seemed that her precious son had helped himself to our precious kitchen stores and there was a bit of a 'stand-off'.

We resorted to spending a lot of time in our room, we only emerged to cook and eat meals.

This was not a good situation for anyone, and we started to search for somewhere else to live. This was very difficult and desperate, especially in winter.

Holiday flat

After a little searching, we found a holiday flat in Dawlish. This is a lovely area in the summer, but everything is bleak in the winter, including the people, who are not so welcoming out of season. However, with wellington boots and waterproof coats, life can still be an adventure!

Although we had a roof over our heads, we were still homeless. We had no security, no income and no idea what our future held. The pressure was intense. Peter's distress was high during these times of homelessness. This was a great concern to me. These were hard times and Peter felt like he was under huge pressure. He felt distressed at every situation – about where we would spend the night, where we would find welcome, where we would live, where we could go next and how we would get there. Unbeknownst to us, Peter's twin sister, Holly had been strongly campaigning on our behalf to their dad.

The wilderness

In 1973, to improve our circumstances and relieve some of the pressure, Peter's dad offered to buy us a house in Saffron Walden. He thought it would be better to be closer to one another, so we could offer each other support when needed.

A house was found and bought, and we moved in.

At this time Peter used to say that he felt like we were entering the "wilderness". He never said what he meant but I was expected to understand.

The house was a good house and it was in a reasonable area. This was a great opportunity to make a go of leading a healthy and settled life, but Peter's feelings of the "wilderness" prevailed. The ideas of the "wilderness" – bleak, dry and arid – led to us regarding everything in our lives with negativity. We made it the "wilderness".

Even here, somewhere new, a fresh start, we instead continued to be very suspicious of everyone and of all our neighbours, therefore increasing our isolation. Even so against all the odds we did stay for three and a half years.

Whilst we lived in Saffron Walden Peter's dad visited us regularly and we would go and see him every Saturday. He was keen to continue to show us his support and help us in any way he could. He was very kind and supportive to us, especially to Simon.

We made our time at Saffron Walden as fun as we could for Simon, and we strove to find opportunities for him to learn. We did a lot of truck spotting; we investigated the sugar beet factories and we explored disused railway lines.

It was at this time that Peter's dad supplied *'Farmers Weekly'* to Simon as a source of inspiration. We spent time writing about many things, including Louisiana, where our friend Ben from the American Air Force lived. We learnt about many other countries, farms and machinery. It was an area with lots of arable farming, so it was the perfect time of year to learn about these topics. There were plenty of combine harvesters about to enjoy and delight in.

The countryside was beautiful, especially the picturesque duck pond at Finchingfield and there were many existing windmills to admire. We visited a windmill conversion owned by a lady who attended St Pick's Church, which was local. She had converted the windmill into a lovely home, which we were very impressed by.

The wilderness continued

Although we did our best to ensure we were making full use of everything around us, we continued to not feel welcome. Simon was getting that little bit older and the signs and symptoms of Cri du Chat were becoming more evident in Simon's appearance, communication and behaviour and sometimes the reactions of others would be hurtful. We often found that people, both children and adults, would stare at us. For instance, children who were in front of us, out with their parents, would start to walk backwards so they could stare at us whilst they were licking their ice cream.

Actions like this would really upset me and at first, I was not sure how to react. I would feel uncomfortable, protective, angry, insecure and resilient all at once, a difficult mix of emotions to work out how to balance and act upon.

I would become very confused and I didn't know how to respond appropriately or in a manner that would not reveal the incredible amount of anger and distress I was feeling.

Sometimes I could feel so violently provoked and angry that I felt ashamed.

Staring hurts

When people stare it really hurts. It still does; this has never gone away. I find that now children still stare, and I am still fiercely defensive.

In my experience the children who appeared to be from more privileged backgrounds were often the ones that stared and appeared to judge more than other children. Children who appeared to be from more modest backgrounds were often kinder and more sympathetic, perhaps because they too had suffered.

It was only when I reached the age of 40 that I was given a wonderful tip that works well – smile and wave persistently until they respond! They may wave, or they may stop staring and look away or they may smile a lovely smile that melts my heart!

We were an object of curiosity for people to stare at and also the focus of inappropriate and insensitive remarks.

It was also hurtful when people or children noticed us and visibly shrank to avoid us or would look around for a place to get out of the way.

All these experiences contributed to our feeling of isolation from other families and other people.

Avoiding people

We loved Simon passionately and we wanted nothing but the best for him. We distanced ourselves from people who disagreed with us, didn't understand us, were negative towards us, or hurt us.

Peter continued to be disconnected and isolated; he made no efforts to establish relationships and actively avoided contact with other people.

He went to great lengths to avoid making contact with people; he even washed our car away from the house in a quiet spot near fords and streams because he didn't want to do it with people around.

In the evenings Simon went to bed early and I painted flowers on greetings cards, flowers that I had found on our frequent walks in Essex. I also sewed clothes and became very expert with a needle.

Although life was very much more settled than it had been for a long time, Peter still struggled to maintain a positive outlook on life, and he struggled with negative thoughts. Even though Peter's dad had been a huge source of support, Peter began to distance himself. We eventually stopped visiting Peter's dad. Peter had become suspicious of his Dad's third wife and did not wish to spend time with her.

As an alternative to these visits we instituted our own treat and called it "Super Saint Simon's Tea". This served as a suitable alternative for Simon and prevented him from becoming distressed about not seeing his loving, doting grandad.

We didn't treat Peter's dad very well; we did not appreciate him.

Peter's dad had voiced his thoughts and opinions on our lifestyle and what we needed to do as a family to improve our lot. We felt that the path we were wishing to take was the right one even if this was against Peter's dad's opinion and judgement.

Hospitalised

Peter had become more antagonistic and had begun exhibiting increasingly bizarre behaviour at home. This unusual behaviour included drumming loudly at night and becoming aggressive and threatening towards the neighbours. Peter's sister, Holly, visited, and we could hear Peter upstairs practising ministering against sorcery. I had rows with Peter's dad because he called the psychiatrist and the police. At this time, when all this was happening, Simon was just 10 years old.

It all got too much for Peter and in 1975 he was hospitalised. Over time, Peter was hospitalised at least a dozen times in at least three different hospitals.

This period of hospitalisation and involvement from professionals drew attention to Simon. They got involved and, as we had originally suspected when Peter first lost his job, felt that he ought to be at school and 'in the system'.

Exiting from the wilderness

After a three-week stay in hospital Peter was discharged and he returned home.

At that time (1976) we did make a good friend in Saffron Walden. He was called Mr Pickering and he was the pastor at a local tiny church. Simon called him "Saint Pick" and he visited us frequently; we enjoyed each other's company. He was nice company, reassuring and not at all judgemental.

Although Peter was now at home, he was refusing to take the medication he had been prescribed whilst in hospital. This was another indication that Peter was in complete denial of the facts – regarding his mental health or any other facts about his life.

Peter had started to voice dissatisfaction with the house in Saffron Walden. Among our complaints was the fact that the walls were paper thin. The faults we found with the house were beyond Peter's dad's abilities to rectify. Looking back, we could have made the house nice and pleasant if we had wanted to. The problems were with us and not the house. Peter's dad temporarily rented a lovely place for us at Chideock, which was by the sea. We had a lovely time roaming the beaches where we found fossils. We enjoyed seeing bullfinches in the trees outside the bedrooms and the early camellias in the garden.

The house had a fabulous big garden and there was a wood burning stove, which was an enjoyable challenge and so was the electric cooker, which we used to make lots of lovely food and treats. I discovered how to make sponge cakes on top of the stove!

In winter Peter used to bring me in camellias to put in my hair. This was really thoughtful, and it made me feel lovely. This was wonderful and it was the first time in a long while that we had all been at ease and able to live without worry, stress or concern. We were all relaxed there. We had fun days out. Our favourite place to go was Brideport, visiting the sea and the port or looking for fossils at Charmouth. We also visited the surrounding areas and spent time on the Jurassic coastline.

Whilst we lived at Chideock we attended a tiny fellowship of Plymouth Brethren. The minister was very kind to us, as they all were. There were about six people in the congregation and the room that he rented for the Fellowship meetings was so cold that you could see your breath on the air, but the company was kind and the atmosphere warm.

The minister used to visit us where we were staying, and he would bring us boxes of chocolates, all with just a few taken out. I think his congregation may have given them to him, but he didn't really want them.

Winter shutdown

People in the West Country are so kind and welcoming in the summer, but in winter we found they closed in, the number of visitors reduced, and the atmosphere changed. The people were no longer welcoming, the shops were closed, and the people that remained there did not want anything to do with us. It seemed that yet again our life was about to embark on a downward spiral as it also became clear that the estate agent wanted to get us to leave earlier than the agreed six months.

Unbeknownst to us, there was another drama unfolding – Peter's dad had decided to desert us in Chideock. We were not at all aware of it; however, Peter's twin sister, Holly, was very militant on our behalf and campaigned and forced her Dad not to abandon us. She had been our champion.

Towards the end of our stay in Dorset Peter's dad softened and offered to buy a house on our behalf in Bradford but he wanted us to go and choose it.

A snap decision

In 1977 we started looking for places to live in Bradford. We had viewed a few houses and we were unable to make a decision. Peter's dad was keen to arrange a purchase quickly, so we arranged a two-day house hunt.

We stayed in the Cartwright Hotel in Bradford for two nights so we could see a number of properties in one visit.

We had shortlisted the houses down to three, and we decided to return to these properties to check on the natural daylight as we wanted as many windows and as much natural light as we could.

Having second viewings on a few properties and having a clearer idea about what we wanted helped us make a decision and we chose our new home on Clifton Place in Shipley – it won by a long shot. The property is an end Victorian terraced house and there is a wonderful amount of natural lighting with large windows and extra windows on the gable end; it gets sun all day. The property was purchased, and we made all the necessary arrangements to move into our new home in early 1977. That move was our final move and we settled into our new home, which became our home for life.

Account book

When we moved into our new home, we wanted to make sure that we would be secure and kept out of trouble. We started to keep a closer account of our finances and we kept a clear and detailed account book.

We also met Martin Robinson soon after we moved into Clifton Place, who became a long-standing friend. He was presenting his magnificent and grand steam roller at a community event in Lister Park, which is over the road from where we live. This marked the start of Simon's enthusiasm and lifetime passion for all things steam, engines and machinery. On this occasion, Martin had been watching from a distance and when we approached, he said: *'I've been watching those louts make fun of you and if they'd have been any more trouble I'd have come over and thumped them.'* Good old Martin.

On moving to Shipley, we started to attend the Apostolic Church. We were welcomed for a while and we were pleased that we had found somewhere to worship, but it did not feel like the right church, so we kept searching and in 1978 we found the Church of God of Prophecy, a church that drew in the West Indian community. This was a very welcoming church and we would enjoy good food together with all the families, including chicken, rice and peas on a Sunday. This became one of our favourite meals which we still enjoy today.

During this time, we used to go for long afternoon drives in the countryside. We often went in the direction of Haworth and when we got there, we would look over the railing at the fire station where we had a good view of the steam trains.

No welfare

Up until Simon reached 12 years of age, we never claimed anything that we would have been eligible for. We didn't access support, benefits or professional input. We were afraid of what people might do to us or expect from us.

In 1977 we also started to receive child benefit for Simon at £28 per week and the attendance allowance (the state benefit paid to people living with learning difficulties or disabilities in the UK who need constant care at home, for which we received £134 monthly).

We did not visit the doctor so they had no involvement as, again, we were concerned as parents that a GP might alert the local authorities of our situation and we did not want them getting involved and breaking up our family unit; we were worried about contacting the local authorities, scared of everyone around us.

When Simon was poorly, we wouldn't call a doctor. Instead, we would pray, Peter and I would take care of him and we would seek spiritual guidance. I would use the knowledge I had gained during my nurse training and I would care for Simon in the best way I could.

Peter's dad continued to support us, and he would send small amounts of money which was extremely generous and much needed as we had no financial support from other sources.

The small budget we had also had to stretch to "material fents", which are small fabric remnants which I used to make Peter's trousers and to sew and mend our clothes.

On the up

We had settled into our new home and our finances were beginning to look better; in January 1979 our bank balance was £1,722.68, much better than it had been for a long time and at least we were comfortable. Peter had a legacy from his stepmother, his dad's third wife, and proved himself, with the aid of financial advisors, to be competent at increasing the amount of assets.

At this time Peter embraced a new interest, French polishing, in which he became a skilled perfectionist. He did his research and bought his equipment through mail order. He would spend hours rubbing the furniture down gently and he gradually applied thin layers of varnish. Peter enjoyed this pastime; he found it calming and he could see the rewards of his efforts and labour. A lot of the furniture in our home has been French polished by Peter and it all looks top notch with a fantastic finish.

I was also very homely during this period. I made lots of jam and marmalade, baked cakes and cooked. I designed and made waterproof full-length cagoules for our wet walks to make sure we could keep going and keep dry when striding over the moors in winter.

Peter's dad continued to help us out. He generously paid the car insurance to make sure we could keep on the road. He also paid for a full set of Encyclopaedia Britannica, 20 copies in total, and these proved invaluable in our lessons with Simon as we continued to educate him at home. This was before the internet and so there was no searching Google to find information.

Two religious nuts

Although we were much more settled and comfortable and home life had improved greatly, we still went through difficult times. Peter was still struggling with his state of mind, his paranoia and negative emotions. When we went shopping Peter would worry and felt anxious. He would be concerned about other people's judgements and about money. We had to stick to a tight budget of £30. He would become so anxious that it made him stay up all night to "keep away the demons", then the sleep deprivation would add to the problems.

At this time, I was still estranged from my parents and I had not seen them for a very long time. They had no idea about what we had been through – the constant moving, the insecurity, the distress and Peter's hospitalisation. My parents had been to visit Peter's sister and she told me about how my mother was sitting in tears. It was then I realised that this was dreadful; it had to change.

Self-imposed siege

We had been through a long period of time where we had created blockades around us which helped to challenge and defend us against the outside world.

This self-imposed siege happened again much later in the early 1980s, while we were living in Clifton Place. We would only leave the house for essentials, and we would not venture out for any other purpose; we would not talk to people or make contact with people we knew.

It was a very sad situation. There must have been many kind people around us, who didn't know how to get through to us – people who were concerned about us, cared about us and whose actions we misinterpreted.

This siege made us antagonistic to our neighbours and we showed no interest in developing or maintaining a relationship with them.

We led a self-contained, self-sufficient life as a small family in our own home.

In many other ways, in our own world that we had created, it was a very full and interesting life and for Simon I made it the best possible life that I could, visiting new places and learning new things. At that time Peter laid down his life for us doing the washing, cleaning, cooking, facilitating Simon's teaching and taking us out.

A great loss

In 1984 we worked hard to manage the money we had available to us and things were looking much better financially for us. By then we had £6,617.26 in the bank – a much more secure position and this provided us with reassurances and comfort.

At the same time, we suffered a great and sad loss as Peter's dad became very ill and passed away. He had been our one consistent and reliable supporter and had been there for us that year through the most difficult and trying times.

In his will he left us £14,000, which continued to support us into the future but could not replace him and his kindly presence in our lives.

A big confrontation

Our lives were much more financially secure, but Peter's mental health continued to be unstable and in 1985, his antipathy to the neighbours accelerated and, after a big violent confrontation, the police were called.

He was admitted to Scalebor Park Hospital, a mental health institution, and I was also sent there for "observation". Completely against his will,

Simon had to go to live at Drapers' Hall, a respite service, to which he had never been before.

At the hospital Peter was upstairs on the men's ward, in solitary confinement and under guard, and I was downstairs on the ladies' ward. The ward I was on was less strict and I had much more freedom. I know this seems odd to say, but I had a good time, a very good time. I was my own person there with only me to consider.

I made lots of friends and I realised that this was the first time in a long time that I had been allowed to have the chance to do so. Whilst at the hospital I had lots of new experiences, such as someone else cooking for me, I had time to explore new interests. I developed new skills and learnt all kinds of handicrafts. I did a lot of sewing and became more skilled in making clothes including a wonderful dress for me to wear to the New Year's party.

Freedom

The evenings were relaxing, and I spent time chatting with my friends. I went to a charity shop, which was in the hospital, and we celebrated other people's birthdays. How strange that the first time I had a sense of freedom in a long time was when I was detained in hospital. What an eye opener!

In many ways it was like a holiday, full of good friends, activities, no cooking meals, no caring, pleasing myself and organising my own life within their confines.

Looking back at these times I realised that I needed this input to deal with the changes and pressures that had occurred in my life. I may not have been able to continue without the time spent at the hospital and the help and support I received from the staff and the other patients there. It was fun! It was OK.

I was having a rest, even though at the time I believed I had been incarcerated.

On admission I was not allowed to see Peter for a fortnight, and after I had made a lot of fuss about our rights, they eventually let me visit him.

Simon had to wait longer to see Peter and then was only allowed to see his dad if he had two other observers present! I really resented how our family was watched constantly. Mine and Peter's relationship was so suspect we had to have two people from the local authority present on visits, the social worker and a worker from respite. As we never had people from the local authority involved in our lives before, their constant presence was frustrating and distressing.

I did a lot of campaigning and pleading for Peter both inside the hospital and after I had been discharged home. Even after everything we had been through and the stay I had had in hospital, I still believed that he was right and that everyone else was wrong. His influence on my life was so strong, he was my husband and I stayed true to the vows I had spoken when we had married.

I was discharged after a month, but I asked to stay on as a voluntary patient, just for a while. I wanted to be with Peter. After a short while as a voluntary patient I decided to return home, after which Peter remained in the hospital for a further six months.

Once Peter was placed in a less secure section and was able to move with greater freedom around the hospital, I continued to visit him. We went to tea dances and evening film shows and walked in the grounds together. Peter also got involved in the activities on offer at the hospital; he did woodwork and other activities in the handicraft shop, which resulted in him making me a very fine dressing table stool, which I have treasured.

As part of my recovery after leaving the hospital I had to have a "case" meeting. I asked for the social worker not to be present as I had come to dislike him and his influence, or his attempted influence. I felt like he had been pushing for us to be more "normal" and to lead our lives in the way that he felt was best. We thought he wanted us to fit in with his cosy social worker ideas of what a family should be like. He had no understanding or appreciation regarding the complexities we faced and how mental health influences your perceptions of life.

Drapers' Hall

As Peter and I were hospitalised at the same time and then due to the pressures on my time and the need to support Peter with his recovery, it was necessary for Simon to live at Drapers' Hall for some time. He made a good effort and seemed to adapt quite well.

When I first visited Simon at Drapers' Hall in 1985, he had very little to do with me. I was reassured by people who told me it is quite normal for children to respond like that when they have been parted from their parents. I believe he was soon okay again.

I phoned him on a regular basis. Once when I phoned, he sounded a bit mournful, I said, *'Simon what's the problem?'* He sighed philosophically and replied, *'You can't get the staff these days.'*

Although Simon made it clear that he wasn't happy there, he showed himself to be resilient and resourceful. He managed the situation and staff brilliantly, impressively and subtly. He appeared to adjust to Drapers' Hall, and he managed to make some good friends there.

He has never liked smoking but he noticed there were a few people who smoked at Drapers' Hall, so he got a NO SMOKING notice and put it outside his door.

Sadly, Simon's habits for reading books and playing with toys and leaving them all over the place resulted in them being torn and destroyed by others, which caused Simon great distress and upset; he would miss the books and toys he had grown to love.

I also fretted for him as he didn't seem to receive thoughtful and considered support. He often wasn't dressed warmly enough and sometimes wasn't even dressed in his own clothes.

He was occasionally poorly, and they didn't seem to know how to look after him properly. For instance, if he had a raging temperature, they thought he needed to be kept warm and well covered when, in fact, a high temperature needs to be brought down.

However, it wasn't all negative whilst Simon was at Drapers' Hall; he had several outings and holidays with his carers, and he enjoyed these. He had lots of fun and made friends and was popular.

Peter returning home

When Peter came out of hospital, we made a point of visiting Simon weekly. Peter continued to feel very wretched and it took a great deal of encouragement to get him there at all.

This was a personally challenging time as I missed Simon dearly and I wanted him home, but I also realised that Peter was not himself.

Prayer again kept me strong. When I look back to these times, I remember how real Jesus was to me; the act of praying and seeking support and guidance helped me a great deal. Prayer gave me the time and the peace to be able to think about the situation and concentrate on finding a solution or direction. I was aware that Jesus was my very close, best friend, and I knew that "Our God is great."

Heaton Royd

In 1987, to increase the financial income for our family, I began nursing at Heaton Royd in Bradford. This was a long-stay hospital for elderly patients. This was a first for me and therefore I began a different learning curve. I had been out of work and out of nursing for some time, so I made time to re-familiarise myself with basic nursing care.

There was one patient from Heaton Royd who clearly stands out in my memory: Martha May, aged 110. She had lived and worked on a farm all her life. She used to sit back, with her eyes shut, in a very superior manner, only speaking occasionally. I remember once sitting down to feed her and she said, *'I am not having mushrooms; they are grown in shit!'* I was completely taken back and amused at the same time at such a remark from a strait-laced lady.

While I was there, we celebrated another patient, Sarah's, 110th birthday and she had a visit from Prince Charles – what a memorable occasion! He crouched/kneeled on the floor to speak to her at eye level – what a thoughtful gesture!

In 1987, I moved from Heaton Royd to Stoney Ridge Hospital, which provided the same type of care. Both nursing homes were only half a mile from each other, so I didn't have a great deal further to travel. It was hard work with lots of heavy patients, lots of lifting, rolling, bathing, feeding, toileting, back care, dressings and doing everything for everybody...at times this was simply exhausting.

In the afternoon, where possible, we tried to make a special effort to dedicate the time to the residents only. We had occupational therapy staff coming in and occasionally we went out on trips on the minibus. Some people had gotten so used to being in the hospital, stuck "in the rut" and routine that we needed to really encourage them to go out. You sometimes would take them out whilst they protested, but they would love it when they got there. The staff team I worked in also had fun together; we cooked meals and celebrated together.

A lady called Marianne, who I cared for at Stoney Ridge Hospital, was a beautiful lady who could not speak. She had been a real rebel in her youth and gone to join the Russian Revolution. She never married; she had a child out of wedlock and brought the child up. She spent all her life campaigning, her last campaign being one against the closure of a hospital. She was said to be an atheist but when I bathed her alone in the bathroom, I would sing hymns and whilst I was singing, Marianne, who couldn't speak, joined in *"Crown Him, Crown Him"*. She could sing, even though she couldn't speak.

Sadly, despite the fun I had with my colleagues and friends, there were several ward sisters at Stoney Ridge who decided to make life very difficult for me. They were unpleasant and rude. Nothing I did was ever good enough and I was ridiculed.

It was difficult to cope with, especially as I worked so hard, but I didn't bring this home with me; we already had enough going on. If I did take anything from work back home with me, it was only to pray about the matter and not to burden Peter or Simon.

Absconding

Although Peter had not been aggressive or violent, he would behave wildly in the house, refused to listen and insisted on keeping both front and back doors open all night while he prowled around. He was on some sort of metaphorical 'high' I suppose, out of control and wild. I asked for help but never got it until eventually I phoned the police. I took Simon to sit in the park over the road and we sat on the bank and waited for the police to take Peter. Around 1990 Peter was hospitalised again at Lynnfield Mount.

On several occasions he walked out of the hospital and "absconded" by walking home. They sent a police van to the house for him and he went back with them quite passively but once there were six police in that van! They had arrived heavy-handed and prepared. This was a hard situation to deal with; Simon was really upset, and I tried to console and reassure him whilst I could also see all the girls in the hairdressers over the road stood staring. How rude! just to stand, stare and gawp! I could do without that. What were they making of the situation? Were they entertained or concerned? Would they avoid me in the future or tell everyone about what they had witnessed?

Further learning

In the early 1990s, whilst working at Stoney Ridge, I heard about a two-year course in orthopaedics in Bradford Infirmary and I realised that I would really love to do it. I approached the relevant people to express my interest and discuss the opportunity and I knew this was right for me, so I applied to go on the course.

I enjoyed orthopaedics and knew this was an opportunity to advance myself and my skills. I was optimistic and I got in! I was overjoyed because no-one had ever had great expectations of me.

This was a complete step out of both my usual nursing world and work that I was used to and my everyday life. It was my opportunity to prove myself, do something I enjoyed and achieve my ambition of progressing further in my nursing career. I knew that some of the ward sisters, who had low expectations of me and had been putting me down, were quite put out by my triumph. At last I was going to do something for myself. I had the chance to say: *'Blow you dearie, I am getting out of here.'*

I started the orthopaedics course and it went so well that it ended up being condensed from two years to six months! So, there was a lot more to do than I expected, and the pressure was higher.

It proved to be another steep learning curve for me. I really had to apply myself as I hadn't studied for over 20 years and I certainly didn't know about modern nursing practice and procedures. I had to pull myself up-to-date in every area. I think I did fairly well. I really took everything on board – I was a sponge and the training was brilliant.

Primary nursing

Upon my successful completion of the course I looked for a job that would allow me to practice my newfound skills and knowledge. At first, I couldn't get a job on the grade I needed to support my family, so I kept trying and after 20 applications I was accepted as a primary nurse in Chapel Allerton, Leeds. It was a big commute from home to work, a 60-mile round trip! This was during a time when Peter was doing very well; he was stable, and he was experiencing fewer negative thoughts or at least he had them under control. Calmer and more content, Peter offered to drive me to work in the car.

This took quite a bit of organising to get it right. We would shower Simon before we set off in the morning to get me there in time for a 7am start. Peter and Simon would go back home after dropping me off and Peter would get Simon ready for whatever he was doing that day (he would help Simon have his breakfast and get dressed into the clothes he needed to wear that day).

At this time, I was never anxious or worried about Peter and Simon being at home together because during this period Peter was on top of things, in good spirits, positive and in good form.

Nursing is not the type of job where you have the brain space to think about anything else other than what you are doing so it had to be this way otherwise, I would not have been able to perform my duties well.

Primary nurse

Securing and learning this job as a primary nurse was, again, another very steep learning curve. I think people really liked me at the interview; I had a brilliant CV, but I needed to learn the job from scratch and required a lot of support at the beginning.

I was keen to continue to develop my skills and understanding as a nurse. I completed several courses as part of my role, and I was always learning. I went on infection control, ENB (English National Board), teaching and assessing and many other one-day and two-day courses. I enjoyed most aspects of my job but found the internal politics sometimes difficult, stressful and distracting.

I had to stop and realise how well I had done – I haven't nursed in 20 years and in a very short space of time I went from being a staff nurse in a long stay hospital to a primary nurse on an acute elderly ward, all thanks to the orthopaedic training I had received and the dedication and commitment I had been able to give. Praise God!

The London trip

When Peter was in and out of hospital, Simon and I would occasionally take ourselves off on trips, much to Peter's dismay. Peter showed no interest during these times in doing anything fun; often he just wanted to stay at home, but I couldn't let this hold back Simon's enthusiasm and zest for life.

Simon and I had a number of lovely adventures together. We had a full weekend in London, where we visited Madame Tussauds. All the visitors were looking very serious; however, Simon went up to all the wax effigies and talked to them and conversed with them. There he fell in love with Lydia
Sharman, the astronaut... or at least the wax version!

We had a hotel room high up overlooking Tower Bridge and we could see the big ships going through. We watched the bridge when it had to be raised. We kept the curtains open all night to see all this, it was so exciting.

Zip wires

We also went on an adventure and activity holiday together in Cumbria. It was designed for people with learning difficulties and offered zip wires, rock climbing and trekking. We were at the muddy water's edge and we had to pull our boots out of the boggy mud...this was not at all glamourous or civilised, but it was messy and a great deal of fun.

I really loved it; I especially liked the zip wires. I think this sense of adventure is in my blood. My mother was very adventurous; I have a picture of her climbing a climbing frame in her eighties.

On this occasion I do not think Simon enjoyed this holiday as much as me, although he could be persuaded to join in, so he wasn't completely put off or unwilling.

Great Yarmouth

On another occasion we had a coach trip Monday to Friday to Great Yarmouth in the winter. This was an interesting time to visit the seaside;

we took our wellington boots and waded through the sand on the beach.

We met a local farmer and later visited him. His son took Simon on an off-road four-wheel drive and Simon was thrilled. He hung his hands out of the window in great delight trying to catch the mud splashes.

Another hospital admission

Whilst I worked at Chapel Allerton in Leeds, Peter was readmitted to hospital and he was no longer at home to help with Simon and to support me to get to work. I had to find alternative transport to get there. I decided to get a taxi there, which cost a lot of money, and public transport to get home, which took 1.5 hours and was incredibly tiring after a full day at work. It was depleting my energy and time.

Over the following few years it became very difficult for Simon and me.

I continued to work at Chapel Allerton. The job I had was high pressure and managing my work demands, offering the support I needed to provide to Peter and manage our home affairs proved too much and eventually poor Simon had to go into intermittent care again and with great difficulty.

It became increasingly challenging for me to continue working, partly because of the travelling time, partly because of the distress about Simon and also because I needed time to visit Peter.

Whilst I was working at Chapel Allerton hospital, I was in charge of a team of nurses who were very supportive, and I really loved and enjoyed being in my team.

Although I was well loved by people in my team, the seniors tried to keep breaking the team up. We would hold team meetings and I'd treat them all to a cream cake. I think the senior managers believed this was a waste of time and not all the teams held team meetings, but we believed these were a good thing, as it helped to boost the team morale, provided a chance to communicate and enabled us to bond.

One Christmas time we had arranged for an entertainer to come to cheer everyone up and share some of the Christmas spirit. We were all excited about this and looking forward to it. We got all our patients ready and sitting out in a large circle. At the last minute the entertainer called to cancel so I stepped in wearing Victorian costume, singing all the old songs that I had learned at Stoney Ridge. It was very successful! They really enjoyed the singsong and nearly everyone joined in.

However good the job was there was still a bullying culture in the hospital. I felt very challenged by the hierarchy. I had done some whistleblowing there, which was really unusual at the time as people tended to turn a blind eye. I had done this with the hope that it would improve matters but unfortunately it didn't, which is often the case when someone whistle blows in an institution of this kind. Due to my approach, the senior managers did not like me, and they re-jigged my team, much to the team's dismay, and eventually my team was disbanded.

At this stage I knew that my job had changed so significantly that it would be difficult to continue to enjoy it and I realised that I must get a new job that was closer to home.

Eventually, after a few months and a number of different interviews, at the end of 1995 I secured a job as a staff nurse at F4 ward at St Luke's Hospital in Bradford. This was an extremely interesting role because it involved dermatology, strokes and rheumatology. I found the job fascinating.

The staff team were lovely and sometimes we would have big parties in the adjacent, empty ward organised by the ward sister and we were applauded by all the patients. We would parade around in our party clothes and patients would enthusiastically get involved. This new job resolved the commuting issue and I was much closer to home – a bus into Bradford and a pleasant walk past the blossom trees up the hill to St Luke's, which would take less than an hour and I could do it myself without needing a lift.

After a year of nursing at Ward E4, in 1996, the sister in charge at Stoney Ridge enticed me to return, which I did. She soon realised this was a bad move as she became aware that I knew more than her and was more professional, due to the training and experience I had received since leaving Stoney Ridge.

My dear friend – emerging

I met up, for the fourth time, with a dear friend of mine, Lydia, when I started working again at Stoney Ridge. This was not planned. She said: *'This is amazing. This is not a coincidence; this is God's plan.'*

Very soon after meeting again she had to convert from a SEN (state enrolled nurse) to RGN (registered general nurse) and needed a mentor. She asked me to mentor her and I agreed. This was a huge vote of confidence!

My new role required lots of my time, a lot of phone calls and a lot of support.

Turning point

Meeting my dear friend again at Stoney Ridge has been a Godsend. It was through my conversations with her and the support she gave me that I was able to regain control of my life and to get back on track... to feel like me again. I thank God for her.

At this stage in my life I had started to do a lot of the things that Peter had not allowed me to do before. Peter was still in hospital and, although this brought with it stresses and strains, it also brought a certain amount of freedom.

I had started to mix with the rest of the world. I got a modern hairdresser, I opened windows and doors without asking for approval (wow!), I also started wearing lipstick and indulging in my love of colour.

These had all been taboos in our life and I needed to break them. Praise God I did; at last I did not feel as trapped as I had, and I was relishing the new life I was building.

This was a significant stage in my life which I could call the "turning point".

It was at this time that I began to realise what had been happening in my life and what had caused my life to become so restricted and controlled.

What an eye opener this was! It had taken 40 years of living a life that was challenging and where I had had to navigate through a complex web of emotions and control for me to realise what had happened and to put this realisation into words:

'My chains fell off, my heart was free!' (Hymnal.net, 2019c).

I felt like I was emerging from a cult – and I was!

Night shifts

My time at Stoney Ridge took a turn for the worse when the sister put me on permanent night duty without consulting me. She didn't like me!

Eventually after six months, following my persistence with my request to be moved onto day shifts, the sister produced a large sheet full of her complaints about me. This came as a shock and thankfully I had a representative from the union. The complaints were so trivial and senseless. For instance, the sister complained that I had allowed the patients to call me "Sister". I had not asked for or encouraged this but often patients can be confused or simply do not understand the difference between the nurse or the sister; it happens to every nurse!

After being presented with the list of complaints I felt destroyed, I felt like giving up and leaving. However, I decided to take a week off and I booked an interview with our local nurse manager at Shipley Hospital, Mary Bay. At the interview I told her what had happened and what the sister had presented to me. Mary simply said: *'She can't do this.'*

Shipley Hospital

Even with the support from Mary it was evident that I could not continue to work at Stoney Ridge Hospital and the local manager set me up to work for three months at Shipley Hospital, at that time a model hospital with very high standards.

By sending me to Shipley Hospital the manager could see if there was any substance in the accusations presented by the sister at Stoney Ridge.

I loved it at Shipley Hospital; it was a nice environment and it was also good for my quest to continue learning as there was always an opportunity to learn a new skill or approach – there were plenty of training sessions and experienced people to learn from.

The love of nursing

What I loved about nursing was going to see a patient who was really distressed about their situation knowing that I could make a difference. I relished achieving a sense of calm and reassurance and seeing the patient's relief. I had the chance to do this whilst nursing at Shipley Hospital. This gave me a great sense of purpose.

At the end of three months nursing at Shipley Hospital, Mary recognised that I was a good nurse and the original complaints raised were proved groundless.

Valued at last!

Obviously, I could not return to Stoney Ridge due to the hostility I would receive from the sister in charge.

From Shipley Hospital the manager sent me to St. Catherine's Hospital in Manningham as a staff nurse. It was a hospital for elderly patients who had been discharged from acute wards at general hospitals and were not quite ready to go home.

Patients came to us for either palliative care or for intensive rehab care in order to get ready to go home or to choose a satisfactory nursing home. This was wonderful for me and, after so many years of unpleasantness from senior managers and being challenged from them all the time, it was wonderful to be really appreciated by the ward managers.

There, at last, I was really valued and appreciated! How wonderful that God should at last grant this in my retiring years! With all my previous experience I was able to bring a lot to the job and to the patients; I was able to contribute and make a real difference.

Our great adventure in Israel

In 1994, Peter planned a wonderful "do it yourself" family holiday for us in

Israel. The trip was definitely not a package tour; we did our own thing and it was a 17-day family adventure! We flew to Tel Aviv and stayed for a few days in a young people's Christian hostel. It was gorgeous there because all the meals were eaten outdoors under a canopy of vines and we just ate and mingled with all the young people. The weather was scorching hot and we were about 10 minutes' walk away from the beach. At that time Simon very much enjoyed the sea. He would go into the water and splash around. We all enjoyed the adventure so much; it was a fabulous memorable holiday. We loved everything about Israel – the sun, the people, the land, the cuisine. It was an amazing success, although this would prove to be the last time that any of us would venture abroad – at least it has been so far, but never say never!

The great downfall

Things began to go downhill soon after our adventure to Israel. Maybe it was the stress of organising a holiday that proved to be too much, but it was always difficult, if not impossible, to know what caused the downturns in Peter's mental health.

Peter was readmitted to hospital. This was very difficult for Simon, and for me as again, I had to manage work, travelling, taking care of Simon and visiting Peter.

I made a real effort to keep Simon's spirits up and during this period of Peter's stay in hospital we would go on coach trips together to Great Yarmouth, London and Bendrig. We stayed strong and managed to get through.

Where should Simon live?

At the time I understood that being at home would be the best for Simon – this is what Simon wanted desperately, as did I. This understanding led to Simon's return home (much to my delight) whilst I worked at Stoney Ridge, after living at Drapers' Hall.

No-one, other than I, knew what was going on at home, Peter was again struggling with day-to-day life. He even found the weekly trips out to see Simon too much. Peter did not entertain the idea of Simon returning home and at this stage he felt that Simon was in the best place – this was not at all like Peter! He had always strongly believed in us staying together as a family and that Simon would receive the best of care and support at home. Peter was in a very bad place and I can only guess what was going on in his thoughts; all I knew was that he wasn't himself and that each day was a struggle.

I didn't think that Peter would ever accept the idea of Simon coming home but I continued to talk to Peter about it and the idea grew on him.

How difficult it had been for Simon

A dear friend, Helen Thornton, who was later employed as Simon's support worker, and her husband, Frank, used to take Simon out when I was working and Peter was in hospital.

When Helen and Frank took Simon for his overnight stays at Drapers' Hall, they would report how Simon didn't want to get out of the car and, when he did get out of the car, how he would then not want to go through the door of the respite place because he hated it so much.

It was a sad ordeal that he patiently endured. Simon simply did not want to be in care or away from home. We became aware of how difficult Simon found it when Helen shared her experience of picking Simon up from there to go on an outing and taking him back afterwards:

'On the few occasions in the past when Simon has had to stay at Drapers' Hall, we would take him out for the day to keep our contact with him. Being out of his comfort zone, his frustration could be misconstrued as disruption. He would be pacing the floor very agitated, obviously unable to show his pain and misery in any other way.

'He could not get to the car quick enough, but once on our way, would calm down and begin to enjoy himself. Having seen this happy personality during the day, taking him back became difficult for us too and his frustration became apparent.

'Being away from family and friends for however short a stay proved that this only adds to Simon's pain'.

Now Simon blames us for this nightmare – all these years at Drapers' Hall.

Bye-bye Drapers' Hall

The people in charge at Drapers' Hall were dismissive of the idea of Simon coming home. It wasn't until Simon had been attacked twice, first by a resident and the second time by a member of staff, that they agreed to ask Simon if he wanted to return home.

So, one Saturday we arranged for the Drapers' Hall manager with our family and some of Simon's mates to go for a drive, a drink and a meal at our family home. During the meal we put to Simon the Big Question: *'Would you like to stay at Drapers' Hall or come home?'*

We fully expected Simon to say that he wanted to stay at Drapers' Hall as it seemed to us that he had made some good mates, he was popular and was beginning to enjoy living there.

To everyone's great surprise, he definitely wanted to return home and that was that!

Simon's return home

It was lovely to have Simon back home and for our family unit to be back intact. We had some pleasant times together, despite life still not being plain sailing, the difficulties we had faced not being over. Peter had various crises which continued to cause distress, especially for Simon. The difficulties for me were how to juggle caring for Simon and Peter alongside working.

Lingering horror

Simon still thinks about those times now, over 20 years later and becomes upset at the memory, using words like, "horror", "grief", "nightmare" and "not a lot of love". He lays it on thick.

He has flashbacks and even now when he has pain, he sometimes cries out *'Jesus, please don't let Simon be taken away again!'*

Leaving and never returning to Drapers' Hall was the end of nightmare for Simon, which had gone on for over 18 years! Simon still now lives with a fear of its reoccurrence and so is adamant that *'he wants to live in this house for ever and ever Amen!'*

Difficult times

Simon can have difficult times, and these have happened more as he has grown older; he does struggle, and he can be very bad tempered and irritable. We now realise that his IBS is the cause of this. When Simon is not in pain, he is very sunny, pleasant and delightful.

More settled years

In 1991, Peter started to study carpentry with Eddie, his college tutor, at New Start, a college which offered free classes in Shipley.

I also started to attend classes there, studying various subjects including local history walks, carpentry, plumbing, electrics and various other skills, which sadly I have now forgotten. It was good fun there and I believe that the choice to close it later was a very short-sighted decision as it provided a great service for local people.

We continued to have many good family outings with Simon. We went to Temple Newsam and steam fairs, including Masham steam fair. We also had a caravan holiday to Filey, which was lovely as we were close to the beach and we had some splendid beach adventures. Peter was driving then so we could go out and about around Filey and it was fun. We visited the Pickering steam fair and went to Bempton Cliffs, where we saw thousands of sea birds nesting on the cliffs – it was a bit smelly and Simon named it "Pongton Cliffs".

Later that year we went to the Nun Monkton and Harwood steam fair. Simon threw himself into everything he loves about steam, the engines, the noise and the people.

At the beginning of August, we would all trek up Hollins Hill and stand waiting by the wall for the Trans Pennine run of Old Crocks. They came chugging up the steep hill from Manchester to Harrogate and we cried with delight every time we spotted another one.

Independent Living Fund

By the time Simon was in his mid-thirties we had started to access funding through the Independent Living Fund. We utilised this funding to employ Helen and Frank, Simon's dear friends, as support workers. They were fabulous and supported Simon to go horse-riding as well as on other fun ådventures. Employing them meant an evening and weekend alternative to respite care at Drapers' Hall. Instead, Simon could enjoy days out with other people.

We learnt from Helen and Frank how important it is for people supporting Simon to understand his reactions to situations. All Simon's behaviour is his way of communicating to people how he is feeling, when he is comfortable and when he isn't.

A good support worker would recognise and learn how to respond to Simon in such a way that enables Simon to have some control over his day-to-day experiences and choices.

Helen said: *'We need to understand what makes him tick and work with Simon to achieve that.'* I also remember my friend Lydia once stating: *'He's not a child – he's an adult, so don't be condescending.'* These words stay with me today. It was the first time I had experienced someone advocating for my son as strongly as I had done for all these years – what a breath of fresh air!

Simon tried going to a theatre company for adults with learning disabilities in Bradford, but he hated everything about it. It was thought that attending would help Simon with his communication skills, but unfortunately, he did not take to it at all, and they did not try to use him in the production.

Peter had become an excellent cook and he had mastered some tasty new dishes. He used a lot of cream, wine and other lovely ingredients and he made delicious fruit cakes at Christmas time; he made lots of festive foods as well as some exotic delights. We all enjoyed the finished products of Peter's efforts in the kitchen.

Peter was confident about the house and made a great house husband as well as a capable organiser. At the time he coordinated everything: holidays, appointments, shopping, cleaning, supporting Simon during the evenings, and he was an excellent gardener and a brilliant driver; he did everything! Meanwhile, I worked to bring an income into the family home.

The fearful threat that happened after the fiercest storm

The fear of local authorities and their presence in our lives has never really gone away. Whenever we have had involvement from social workers, nurses or any other professional I have always felt an anxiety about what they may do. I always believed that they could make decisions that would significantly affect our home life; decisions that we would have no control over.

Although I always feel these anxieties, I have found some professionals' input to be really useful; it hasn't always been a negative experience. We have been supported in gaining benefits and funding for support.

My first reaction when a new professional gets involved is always going to be one of anxiety and fear. This is due to some of the negative experiences we have had as a family that have shaped my opinion and also a result of hearing the numerous stories from other families regarding their experiences and what they have had to go through and be up against.

One day I was out with a dear friend of mine, Ellie. We had gone to Skipton for the day. It was a lovely day and, whilst we were out, I told her about the content of some recent social services visits. Social Services had been involved in our lives from the time when Simon started to attend day services, which had been for over 7 years. The involvement from Social Services had not always been a positive experience for Simon or us. Based on the content of the recent conversations with Simons Social Worker, Ellie became very concerned about the intentions of social services. She is a professional within the health and social care field, working in a care home and I am confident in Ellie's knowledge and experience. She told me that social services do have the authority to override Simon's wishes in certain circumstances and this naturally filled me with fear.

After the day out, I made time to have conversations with two other friends who have experience of the health and social care sector. I was filled with the full horror of what these social services meetings could mean for Simon when my friends confirmed that Simon's wishes could be overridden.

I became full of fear, apprehension, forebodings, dread and sorrow. I tried to prepare what I would say and who I could involve in order to resolve the situation.

In despair, distress and disbelief I sent out a text to twenty-six friends...I only stopped at "M" in my phone contacts when I ran out of time.

It read: *'I am full of fear as social services think Simon is in danger of abuse and will watch over us like hawks with the possibility of removing him xx.'*

I had some very positive replies, including one from the pastor from the church we attended: *'If they make any suggestions or imply anything. If they threaten you in any way, please just let me know and we will meet with them. Please do not be in fear you are not on your own. You have a big God and a big family behind you, thank you for keeping me updated'.*

I felt reassured and going through this incident drew me closer to God. I felt assured that: *"being confident of this, that he who began a good work in you will carry it on to completion until the day of Christ Jesus."* (Philippians 1:6).

Simon's place to live, personal budget and new and refreshing ways to do things

In 1992, Simon started to receive a personal budget from the local authority, which was topped up by the Independent Living Fund. We used this funding to help get Simon the right support. We achieved this through engaging with a local support agency as well as employing people directly as support workers for Simon.

At this time Helen Thornton was employed directly by us as a support worker. Helen was brilliant, and she could see Simon's potential. Helen would continue to support Simon to learn and they would have fun over words. She once told me: *'We laughed a lot after his Italian holiday and all our words used to end with "ione", he loved that.'*

Independence and a personal budget

An increase in funding allowed respite for Simon. It took some juggling but eventually, when he couldn't go back to his usual respite place, Drapers' Hall, we were advised to visit a house that dealt with assisted living.

So, we went to visit the place, on a dark, gloomy, foggy night by taxi. The house was miserable and dim. We were shown all around it but from the start of the visit to the end, Simon howled, moaned, and cried with anguish. I realised I couldn't let it happen to him again. "Enough is enough!" Regardless of the expense, I took unpaid carers' leave, until Peter returned home.

'Feath' – getting along with support workers

Simon has always used his own language and for him *Feath* means *friend*. Simon started to get out and about much more without us. He spent time with Les 'Feath' (a nickname that Simon gave her) and he was doing all sorts of interesting things. He also learnt new computer skills. Peter had met Les whilst shopping at Grattan's Warehouse and Outlet and he invited her to work with Simon, which she did very successfully. Les had qualified as an art student but could not find work in this field so Peter advised her to do her nurse training, which she did successfully and, after gaining her qualifications, she secured a job in a residential home, but she eventually left as she felt they didn't listen to new ideas and always gave her the worst off-duty work hours. So, Les Feath went to work for the British Epilepsy Association in Leeds.

Simon also had a German support worker called Petra and she taught him to speak and understand the German language. Petra said that: *'Simon is better at learning German than I am at learning English.'*

In 2001, we had contact from the learning disability commissioner for Bradford and the manager from the agency that provided support to Simon. Simon continued to not enjoy his experience at the day service at Legrams; the support they were able to provide him was very patchy and unsatisfactory.

Often, Simon would come home from the day service very unhappy and stressed, therefore we all were unhappy.

We talked about the possibility of Simon receiving one-to-one support as an alternative to going to the day centre. At this stage we were already accessing the Independent Living Fund and we were able to increase the funding Simon was receiving for his support to make this possible.

When we received the additional funding

Simon started to have support workers coming in three times a week during the day and in the evening. This worked so much better for Simon; he could then decide what he wanted to do and where he wanted to go, and he would be supported to achieve it. He had much more freedom and control.

Simon has had many great support workers and some of them remain his good friends, especially the people who made the effort to ensure that Simon was having a great time and going to visit places of interest to him and places that fascinated him. The good support workers were friendly, chatty and prepared to talk to anyone when out and about with Simon. They appreciated and respected Simon for the funny, intelligent and adventurous man he is and shared the same interests and passions as him.

Church on the way

During another hospital admission for Peter in the year 2000, Simon came with me to Church on the Way. During the service, Simon was very noisy and difficult, and I found this really distressing. Halfway through the service we came out and away from the church and I thought *'I'm never going to do this again,'* but I later learnt that upon our exit, the pastor had led the congregation in prayer for us.

Praise God! Since then, Simon has never looked back and he is well accepted and loved there and there is no way that Peter could ever stop him going. The congregation truly appreciate his faith and enthusiasm for the Lord.

A true Christian

Simon is a lovely Christian. The moment that he hears that someone has a problem he wants to pray for them. If they are sick, he hovers his hand over them and says, *'they are angel wings'* as he makes a wing movement with his hands. His prayer is effectual.

Auntie Nen

In the mid-90s I had decided to get in touch with my aunt, my mother's sister. I used to save up one-pound coins and phone her secretly from a callbox when Peter had no idea what I was doing. This went on for a long time without Peter being aware that I was in fact back in contact with my family.

My aunt, then living in Sidmouth, had always been supportive and had once sent me £5,000, which I never mentioned to Peter. I put this into a separate bank account from which I paid a monthly amount to World Vision, an international charity that supports children around the world who are in need. The organisation provides medical support, water and education on growing vegetables and materials for local schools.

Making contact

After a while I said to Auntie Nen that perhaps I ought to get in touch with Mum and Dad.

I trembled a bit at the thought; I imagined my dad would be recriminating and very angry that I had been out of touch for so long and that he would still be upset about how I had treated them when Peter and I had made the decision to break contact with them.

I did eventually get in touch with them by telephone. I felt so nervous, but everything was okay. We started to have regular chats by telephone, but I still didn't visit them, and these telephone conversations were still taking place without Peter's awareness in secret!

The relationship with my mum and dad was still good, even though we had been separated and out of contact for such a long time. They were overjoyed that I had got back in touch and they eventually opened up and told me that they had thought that I had been abused. Of course I had been in a way, because the relationship I had with Peter was completely controlling. They tried to forgive Peter but, more importantly, they were so pleased that we were speaking again.

During that time my sisters had urged me and tried to convince me to find a way to go and visit my parents. She had suggested that we meet halfway, and I had not, until that point, realised it was possible to do the journey in one day.

I had also not attempted this as I would be doing it without Peter's knowledge, which could have led to all sorts of complications! What if the train was cancelled? How would I explain that? It was too much for me to comprehend.

A few years after making contact with my parents again I was waiting in the train station for a day out with my friend, Faye; we were going to Hebden Bridge. Whilst I was there, I looked at the train timetables and realised – 'yes!' I could get down to see my family in Whitstable and back in one day – wow! This is what spurred me on to arrange a journey to see them after all this time, after 30 years!

At last I found the courage to tell Peter. He was not very pleased, but he had to accept it. This was early 2000 and I was getting bolder; I felt confident and able to tell Peter what was important to me and what I wanted.

I made arrangements, put all the plans in place and made my journey down to Whitstable in Kent.

Thirty years is a long time and people's appearance can change a great deal in that time, but I had seen recent photos of them, so I knew them as soon as I saw them.

When I got off the train, they were there waiting for me at the station.

To see them after so much time was so emotional. We had lots and lots of hugs. We went for a meal at the Oyster Café, their favourite restaurant, and we were overjoyed. After the meal I was invited back to their flat to spend more time together.

I didn't have a lot of time with them; I arrived at 12.30pm and I had to be ready to leave at 3.30pm to make the journey back in one day. After this visit to my parents I realised that they were not the people I had known or left behind 30 years ago. They were more tolerant and more forgiving; they were kinder and calmer.

An emotional realisation

I realised what a precious gift my family were, and what a huge mistake I had made to spend so much time apart from them. I would never be able to get the time back and I grieved for the time we had lost.

My sister Katy

I read a book that my sister, Katy, had written about our family. The book contained her research, including details she had lovingly gathered and recorded. Upon reading Katy's book, I realised that I had left a family that loved being together, that cared for one another and was loyal when I married Peter. My actions had created a huge hole in an otherwise strong family.

Peter had influenced my relationship with my family greatly. He had experienced a very unhappy upbringing as a young child when his Mum abandoned them and later blamed his father, he went through emotional turmoil and this led to him disliking families. He wanted to keep his distance from his own family...and mine. As his wife I thought he knew best.

Wonderful journeys to Whitstable

Whilst my parents were still alive, I used to take myself off on my own and go to visit them. I loved the freedom of the journey to Whitstable, Kent. By this stage, my parents had moved into a Methodist residential home in Whitstable. This was a lovely home for them; there was a fantastic view out to sea. The clouds and sea colours were always changing. Forty steps led down to the beach huts and wide promenade. There was lots of activity including windsurfers and kites and there was always a lifeguard on the beach in a yellow and red hut. The lifeguards were there because of "The Street", which was a wide ridge of sand that ran out to sea at low tide, at the meeting of the water from the Thames and the water of the English Channel. It was a really unsafe area for swimming.

Every two months I would get up early on a Wednesday morning to catch the early train. It was lovely to be free, independent and on my own. It would be one of the rare occasions where I only had myself to take care of. Of course, I thought about Simon and Peter whilst I was away and I was concerned that they would be okay together, but during these journeys and visits to my parents I could relax, have a break and enjoy being my own person.

Whilst I was travelling, I would have time to catch up on things, enjoy the scenery out of the window, listen to music and let the time pass by.

When I arrived in Whitstable I really appreciated and loved the views. I would go to the cliff top and sit there overlooking the sea and sky. The famous Whitstable Oysters are there and therefore lots of shellfish.

The day out to the seaside was so wonderful and therapeutic, I found this view and this place by the seaside blissfully calming and comforting. I still have this view on my laptop screensaver as a reminder of these good times, but now my parents have died I do not have the opportunity to go down there and visit. I really miss these occasions and I really miss them.

When I have talked to people about my journey to Whitstable they have said, *'you must be glad you don't have to do that long journey anymore'.* I don't think they really understand. They seem to think that this must have been a burden on top of all the other things I had to do, but in fact, I really miss it. This was my respite, my break, my family time, my bit of "me time," and what I believe gave me some strength to continue and keep hold of my own sanity.

Long Term Treatment for Peter

Peter was still experiencing a complex level of mental health issues and for him to be released from a hospital setting and returned back home, a Section 117 was put in place and Peter had to agree to receive a fortnightly depot injection. This injection began to be administered in 2002 and it was then passed as a legal requirement for Peter to receive the injection and he was receiving the highest dose of this. Since receiving the injections Peter has not been re-hospitalised.

Retirement

I retired from St Catherine's in 2003. At first, I missed it and went back to visit the patients twice a week, but I had also made lots of plans for all my activities as a retired person. (I discovered sadly, bit by bit, that I was unable to achieve what I had planned as my time continued to be consumed by the care Peter and Simon needed). I had a long list of things I wanted to do – calligraphy, art classes, bell ringing, rambling, study courses, choir and more.

To this day there still lies in the attic an unused recorder and calligraphy set. Although I loved being at work – the other people, the banter, being around the other girls – I have always liked being at home, making a home and I love cooking.

My confession

I often feel overwhelmed and distressed by a full diary, demands on my life and Simon and Peter's demands and noise...the traffic noise...I feel jealous of retired folk who have it easy and have a pleasant life and do nice things – I feel bitter and depressed. This is my confession; most of all I take this to the Lord in prayer.

The evangelist and author Joyce Meyer once heard about someone who went to their pastor and said: '*I hate myself I just hate myself.*' He replied: '*Who do you think you are? You are God's handy work. You are fearfully and wonderfully made. How dare you say that?*' Then I realised that because God has a perfect plan for my life how dare I complain? I am not a mistake and my life is not a mistake and God has a good plan and purpose for me.

Mystery weekend

During 2003 Peter, Simon and I went on a mystery weekend coach trip. This is great fun as you have no idea where you are going; you have to guess. It is a great delight to wonder about your destination right up until the last minute *'I wonder as I wander!'*

Fred Dibnah

In 2004, Fred Dibnah, a great hero of Simon's, died. Simon was saddened by the news, but he kept repeating the line, *'Jesus took Fred Dibnah.'* However, I said: *'We don't know this – it is up to Jesus to decide that.'*

Plenty of adventures

The following year Peter, Simon and I had the time for several coach trips. We went to Edinburgh and The Viking Anglo Saxo Weekend in York and Simon went to Nostel Priory with his friend Marie as there was a traction engine show there. He saw Tall Ships with his friend Brett, including Captain Cook's ship where a kind sailor man helped Simon onto the ship. We also visited the National Coal Mining Museum, but Peter and Simon didn't like going underground; we preferred the engines left around outside instead.

In 2005, Peter, Simon and I had the opportunity to visit Bakewell, which we thoroughly enjoyed – a real Bakewell tart from Bakewell is out of this world!

Beamsley

During this period in our lives we had been taking summer holidays at Beamsley, breakaway holidays for people with physical and learning disabilities.

The building that we stayed in was physically well adapted and there was support available for everyone.

Beamsley was a converted old church sliced in half so that upstairs was a huge recreational room with magnificent views of Beamsley Beacon and downstairs was a corridor with bedrooms going off it.

We went together. It was costly, but it was cheaper for us as I went along as a "volunteer". I enjoyed it because I love to be alongside other family carers and caring for other people apart from my own family. I thought it might be a good environment for Peter to mix in as well. However, Simon and Peter didn't really enjoy it; in fact, they hated it because they didn't have my full-time attention!

I persisted for some years; we had some good outings in a minibus and enjoyed having our food cooked for us by a cook in the evenings. Apart from that, Simon and Peter largely looked after themselves and did not make the most of the opportunity to spend time with others.

A lovely cleaner

In 2007 I employed a cleaner – what a great relief! This was a huge weight off my mind and meant I could concentrate my efforts on taking care of Simon and Peter.

On trial – the fiercest storm

Late 2008 was a time of great difficulty for our family as we feared that Simon would be taken away from us. One of his support workers from the agency had raised a concern which led to a safeguarding investigation.

My local carer's support worker helped me during this difficult time and their support and knowledge was invaluable. I do not know how I would have coped without them. It was an exceedingly stressful time but my memory of it is not clouded, as I recorded it all in writing in my own personal journal as it was happening.

We were facing our biggest nightmare – the fear that most parents of children with disabilities carry; it had been suggested that Simon could be taken away from us.

On 17 October 2008 Simon's support worker stated: *'Simon is self-harming at the moment and that could land you in trouble that is quite serious. We ought to be concerned about Simon's head banging and that he seems more bothered about getting home these last few months. Is he worried or upset about something?'*

This support worker also mentioned that the number of times he had to *'stop Simon from picking himself had increased.'*

'The observation of self-harm and anxiety leads the support workers to believe Simon is feeling some stress at home.'

This support worker ended the conversation by stating that: *'The situation of self-harm will lead to consequences; social services could get involved in a horrible way. Simon could be taken away.'*

This was a dreadful, awful, terrible threat. I decided that I must keep this to myself and carry the knowledge of this alone and deal with what needed to be done. I could not tell Peter anything about the threat of Simon being taken from us, as I knew it was something he would not be able to cope with and the stress of it could have resulted in him being back in hospital himself.

On 20 October 2008 I received a phone call from the social worker:

'My manager has asked me to give you a ring to ask if you can attend a meeting in regard to some concerns raised by the support agency about your son Simon.'

I then said: *'My advocate would like to know why the support agency handled it like this.'*

A follow-up phone call from the social worker confirmed that they felt that it had been handled badly and that, *'the invitation to the meeting would be about extra support that Simon requires and to ascertain if there is a problem to address.'*

I had a further telephone call from the manager of the social work team; this was *'A BIG APOLOGY.'*

'It wasn't meant to be handled like that. It should have been just an informal chat and not an adult protection referral. It was clear that there was nothing untoward. I want to reassure you and ask you not to worry. This is not going to be a formal meeting, just a chat.'

On 5 November 2008 I had a further conversation with my carer's advocate; she was furious. She said, *'how dare he (the support worker) make the referral to the social work team and adult protection without talking to me first?! People need to hear about how Simon is being supported during the day and the lack of care Simon is receiving for his sores whilst he is in their care.'*

The social worker organised an information and feedback meeting, where everyone who had been involved met to talk about how things had gone and had an opportunity to share their opinions.

On 10 November 2008 I got a further telephone call from the social worker. He wanted to arrange another meeting to share concerns that had been raised by key people involved in Simon's life. The aim of the meeting was to try and understand what had been going on in Simon's life. The social worker said he knew how difficult I must find it. A friend of mine came to the meeting to do the minutes, as well as my carer's advocate and the local carer's Mencap support worker. I had several people to support me during this time.

These meetings that were supposed to be taking place were taking a long time to organise and some of the conversations I was having with social workers were repetitive. The threat continued to hang over my head and I had to wait until all this could be resolved. This went on for about six weeks. I was extremely stressed throughout and did not share this with Peter because I knew how distressed, angry and upset he would get.

I found the whole situation extremely difficult and very stressful. I was looking for reassurance and confidence from the "powers that be" that they recognised that Simon was okay, secure and happy in his home life and that he was being well cared for. I did not receive any of these reassurances from anyone; the worry continued to consume me.

The coordinator of the Mencap carer's support project, called Mandy, gave me advice about the information I had to pull together to present at the meeting – it was like a CV! Fancy, just fancy having to do a CV as a carer after 40 years! How preposterous, demeaning and devaluing, but I knew her advice had the best outcome in mind, so I followed the recommendations I had been given. We decided that my CV needed to highlight:

1. I am very proactive with plans; I do a lot of planning for Simon.

2. My involvement with Bradford Plan U.K. steering group – a project focused on identifying and creating a strong community for adults with learning difficulties run by carers and families.

3. Simon's person centred plan, which is shared with his circle of support and professionals to help inform and involve people. It took 72 hours to create!

4. I am a member and actively involved with the Bradford Learning Disability Partnership Board.

5. I attend Carers Voice meetings.

6. I am a "Partner in Policy Making", having attended a full course of "Sharing the Challenge".

7. My involvement with "Making Space."

At the meeting, six weeks after the original report, Social Services were the first to apologise. The support agency was the last people to apologise.

A positive outcome:

- Simon was not taken away from home.

- It was identified that Simon was self-harming as he was being prevented from doing the things he wanted to do. Peter had refused the request from Simon to go to a steam fair as he was fearful and concerned about Simon's safety, but he didn't see the negative effect this was having on Simon.

- We managed to persuade Peter to let Simon go to the Great Dorset Steam Fair, where he had a wonderful time. In 2009, Simon was away for about five days in all and now he has definitely got the T-shirt. Praise God!

Impact of stress

As a result of this extremely difficult six-week period, my blood pressure went up and has remained up ever since. When I mentioned this to the support worker who had originally placed the initial report, he stated: *'he did not regret his actions and believed he did the right thing'*.

Out of interest, all these behaviours that Simon had demonstrated to prompt the safeguarding investigation still happen now. He is still keen to get home, picks his skin and head bangs, and this happens when he has IBS pain.

Simon does suffer considerably on a daily basis with IBS. Digestive problems are often associated with autism and we believe that the two are connected. The agonising pain of IBS can keep him on the toilet for up to three hours at a time.

Taking second place

It was in 2010, when Simon reached the age of 45, that the local authority recognised that he needed support to have a break away from home in a different way to the usual respite provision (which we had learnt did not work for Simon). The direct payment Simon was receiving was increased so he could begin to have breaks away to the seaside with a support worker. He enjoyed this so much more and it has been a great success for him and our family ever since.

I realise that ever since Simon was born, Peter has had to take second place. Even when Simon is out, there is so much to do arranging appointments, attending meetings, sorting his items, organising medication and dealing with phone calls and paperwork, and when he is in, there is even more to do, but when he goes away for his short breaks (he calls them holidays; people in services call it "respite") I have Peter all to myself and it's wonderful to be able to sit down and talk, and have time for each other. During these times I am able to put Peter first as I used to do when we were dating and after we were first wed.

When Simon is on holiday, Peter and I like to go out for a meal together or go shopping or to a show. We sometimes have a special meal at home with wine and/or a drink at bedtime. We catch up, we're romantic, we laugh, and we have fun. Praise God for such precious times!

Lovely holidays

We continued to have some lovely holidays and in 2010 we had a Christmas trip to the Lake District with Simon. Whilst there we had a train trip and a boat trip in the evening. We enjoyed this so much that we went together for several years. Eventually I was the one to give up on it. I decided that it was too dark, too cold and the lake was too forbidding at that time of year and that time of night.

Romantic holidays

Since 2013 Peter and I have had the chance to go away on beautiful holidays together whilst Simon stays at home with people who support him, and they stay overnight with him in the family home.

Simon loves this time and he often tells me that he feels like the "Lord of the Manor".

This arrangement has worked really well, and Peter and I have had the chance to be a couple again for more than just the odd evening here and there.

These holidays have meant a great deal to both of us; we have had time for each other without the daily slog. We have been able to build some lovely memories doing everyday simple things, relaxing, drinking coffee and eating healthy meals together, eating a picnic, watching the sea and clouds – such beautiful and loving times.

Not the man I fell in love with

The man I married was the finest, a man of integrity and compassion, faithful, constant and loving.

Marriage is a precious institution – it is hard work. The relationship needs to be nurtured daily and continually and tenderly cared for through good times and bad.

The bad times can be a hard winter, but are well worth weathering it through together; believing in each other, for when the warm summer of your marriage returns you will be even closer.

I know (and I have verified this with other married couples) that if I were to line up ten of the most eligible and excellent men (among them Peter) that I would still choose my Peter, because he is the finest person - the finest. He laid down his life for us.

Over many years of marriage we had periods that were full of stress and mental health problems and many hospital admissions, which we went through together.

We all change a little in time and married people change together and adjust to each other. No he is no longer the "drop dead handsome" bride groom in our wedding pictures but I am always his "beloved" and he is my "dearly beloved" the true love.

One definition of marriage is "two imperfect people who refuse to give up on one another".

Golden wedding anniversary

Our golden wedding anniversary was in 2013, the 50th year of our marriage. We needed to celebrate and celebrate we did!

Barbara, our neighbour, very kindly offered to cater for us on the premises of her church, the Shipley Baptist, and we sent out all the invitations. However, on the day there was a sudden deep snowfall. When it settled the snow came right up to the window ledges and we had to quickly cancel as there was no way people could get to us especially from Menston or Otley or drive at all, it wouldn't have been safe. Barbara was able to put most of the food into the freezer but there was some that could not be frozen.

We had inspiration and called an impromptu party of very local people in our house. Barbara brought along her delicious food and there were 12 of us that day. Our guests had struggled through the snow to get there but we all had a very pleasant time.

One month later it was my birthday and, although I had wanted to shove the occasion under the carpet and forget it, Barbara felt sure we should have a proper celebration. We hired her hall again, she produced her delicious menu and we celebrated both our golden wedding anniversary and my birthday with close friends, about 30 of us.

Life now?

Simon has achieved more than anyone would have thought possible. He has become a knowledgeable, intellectual, sociable, caring and confident man. He still needs the same level of support, but he is much bigger and stronger as he has grown older; he towers over Peter and me.

Simon has a huge sense of humour and loves to go to church and worship Jesus. He is very compassionate and concerned about other people's needs (if they are explained to him). Simon has arrived at a comfortable and precious relationship with the congregation – they love and accept him and all he gets up to. They also love to hear his loud, heartfelt prayers and feel that he has a valuable contribution to make. It has also been so good for people to discover that they feel easy to the point of losing all embarrassment in communication. It will stand everyone in good stead now, so they will feel confident to communicate with anyone they meet on their journey through life.

We wrote a guide of how to support Simon at church, which is invaluable for those who may support Simon when I am not available.

Simon is also an honorary member of the Leeds District Traction Engine Club. Steam people are a kindly and friendly crew of individuals and they greet us warmly when we go to a steam fair. In 2017 we went to a small, private "steam-up" of about 20 people at Martin Robinson's, a fellow steam enthusiast who Simon met in a local park at home in Bradford. Simon was asking searching questions and he examined everything in detail. It was great because no-one asked me anything about him; they just knew that he knew.

What I love and admire about Simon:

- He has an amazing amount of enthusiasm.
- He is often very sensitive to any needs and distress and will instantly pray about it.
- He is kind and compassionate.
- He responds so well to positivity.
- He loves Jesus and often prays out loud alone.
- He has a huge concern for the salvation of his support workers.
- He is fun and has a lovely huge contagious smile and laugh.
- He brings joy into people's lives.
- He has a photographic memory and absorbs and soaks up facts on all the subjects he is interested in.

- He is not scared to show his passion.
- He praises the Lord jubilantly and his enthusiasm amongst the congregation is catching.

What has kept me strong? How faith supported us through

As a family we have faced testing and trying times. There have been periods of my life that have felt dark and bleak, emotionally challenging where I have had to muster the strength to get by. My love for Peter and Simon has been an ongoing reason to find strength and the support from the friends I have has helped me immensely. The biggest source of strength, love and inspiration has been the Lord Jesus. I love to worship the Lord and to know His strengthening, refreshing, enlightening and comfort.

Many people have prayed for us and are still praying.

We read some good books by Christian authors. They were helpful books, which have proved to be a source of comfort, reassurance and inspiration.

I sang a lot of hymns very loudly and they became songs of deliverance, lifting me out of my "slough of despondency".

God has been and continues to be my refuge and strength, a very present help in trouble.

Prayer feathers

At times when I have been physically and emotionally exhausted it has been incredibly important for me not to lose faith and fall into a desperate, desolate, depressed morass.

When I have felt really desperate, tired and awful, as I would feel after an awful day, I would be the last person to get to bed and I would comfort myself by snacking in the kitchen on puffed wheat.

I would, and still do, text around for prayers and support. I would send the texts to people I knew would pray for me, who I knew were concerned.

This group of people eventually became known as the "prayer feathers", meaning praying friends.

I have often had to urgently text: *'I am having such a terrible time please pray for peace.*

"Prayer feathers" are a group of friends who are available for me to contact to ask for prayer during difficult times. Their earnest prayers prove most effective. God gives hope, strength, encouragement and determination when I need it most. There have been times, numerous times, when "prayer feathers" have been a source of support when Simon's health has been poor and when I have felt insecure and anxious regarding the motivations of the local authority.

References

Hymnal.net, 2019a. What a Friend we have in Jesus. [online]. Available at: <https://www.hymnal.net/en/hymn/h/789> [Accessed 6 January 2019].

Hymnal.net, 2019b. Amazing Grace. [online]. Available at: <https://www.hymnal.net/en/hymn/h/313> [Accessed 6 January 2019].

Hymnal.net, 2019c. And can it be that I should gain. [online]. Available at: <https://www.hymnal.net/en/hymn/h/296> [Accessed 8 January 2019].

Kingsley, EP. 1987 Welcome to Holland

Reading The Gift made me remember all the things I had experienced as a carer. It made me feel incredibly tearful and sad at times, knowing how I had been judged, and how isolated this life was! It made me so emotional, it took my breath away at times.

'This book is a fantastic powerful eye opener! Ann is amazing, warm, funny and loving. God bless!'

Steph Thompson, 2018

Incredible People

Caring Choices

By Mike O' Leary, carer, writer and volunteer

Free to choose
We choose to care
Free to lose
Our losses bear
Free to care
We care for free
Free to gain
From giving freely

Free to starve
Free to freeze
Got no money
Free to sneeze
Free to live
A life unhindered
Food or heating
Fires untendered

Free to live
On dreams and hopes
Free to struggle
Not be cope
Free to think
It could be me
Can't buy a ticket
For 50p

Free to try
To make ends meet
Free to strive
Not be beat
Free to worry
Free to stress
Free to manage
More or less

Free to care
For those we love
Free to give
More than we have
Free to wear
Our good selves out
Free to manage
Just about.

O'Leary, 2017, p.2

People who are family carers have dedicated their life to caring for a loved one and they are incredible People.

A definition of a carer

'A carer is anyone who cares, unpaid, for a friend or family member who due to illness, disability, a mental health problem or an addiction cannot cope without their support.'

Carers Trust, 2015a

'Anyone can become a carer; carers come from all walks of life, all cultures and can be of any age. Many feel they are doing what anyone else would in the same situation; looking after their mother, son, or best friend and just getting on with it.'

Nicholson, 2014, p.2

Family carers don't choose to become carers: it just happens, and they have to get on with it; if they did not do it, who would and what would happen to the person they care for?

When building an understanding of family carers, it is important to recognise what people have experienced and to understand this from their perspective. People do experience very difficult and challenging times, which would affect individuals in different ways. For instance, being drained due to the person they care for constantly demanding their attention or having to face the challenge of a difficult and lengthy bedtime routine for the person they care for whilst being exhausted after a whole day of caring themselves.

With an awareness of how many people in the UK have a learning difficulty it is possible to appreciate how many people are providing care in an unpaid capacity.

'There are around seven million carers in the UK – that is one in ten people. This is rising.

Three in five people will be carers at some point in their lives in the UK.

By 2030, the number of carers will increase by 3.4 million (around 60%).'

Carers Trust, 2015b

"Nothing to do with me!"

Even though there are a great number of people who are family carers, there are an even greater number of people who are not at this stage in their life. For people who are not family carers, however, they often think the situation of caring for a family member doesn't, and never will, apply to them; and when the subject is brought up, they tend to try burying their heads in the sand. For many non-family carers, the subject simply lies outside their comfort zone.

In reality, most people will, at some point in their life, have to care for someone or be cared for but a lot of people do not want to open up their thinking or understanding of this and what it means, unless it is affecting their lives right now.

Lack of support

We were quite isolated when Simon was young; we had minimal contact with other people as our relationships with family members and friends had decreased since Simon was born. We had not contacted our local authority as we were concerned that professionals would come in and take over our lives and we feared that they wouldn't listen to us or appreciate us as a family unit. We were scared of the changes they might enforce or impose upon us.

The fear we felt caused us to avoid any contact with the local authority, who were more powerful when Simon was young, at least they seemed to be.

We were finding it difficult to know how to respond to Simon's behaviour and this was affecting us emotionally and we felt an increased sense of isolation and alienation. Even if someone did have time to listen to us, we would not have been able to articulate or explain our situation.

Autism is a lifelong developmental disability that affects how people perceive the world and interact with others.

Autistic people see, hear and feel the world differently to other people. If you are autistic, you are autistic for life; autism is not an illness or disease and cannot be 'cured'. Often people feel being autistic is a fundamental aspect of their identity.

Autism is a spectrum condition. All autistic people share certain difficulties, but being autistic will affect them in different ways. Some autistic people also have learning disabilities, mental health issues or other conditions, meaning people need different levels of support. All people on the autism spectrum learn and develop. With the right sort of support, all can be helped to live a more fulfilling life of their own choosing.

How common is autism?

Autism is much more common than most people think. There are around 700,000 autistic people in the UK – that's more than 1 in 100. People from all nationalities and cultural, religious and social backgrounds can be autistic, although it appears to affect more men than women.

How do autistic people see the world?

Some autistic people say the world feels overwhelming and this can cause them considerable anxiety.

In particular, understanding and relating to other people, and taking part in everyday family, school, work and social life, can be harder. Other people appear to know, intuitively, how to communicate and interact with each other, yet can also struggle to build rapport with autistic people. Autistic people may wonder why they are 'different' and feel their social differences mean people don't understand them.

Autistic people often do not 'look' disabled. Some parents of autistic children say that other people simply think their child is naughty, while adults find that they are misunderstood.

National Autistic Society, 2016

Reinforcing the fear

The fear we felt was not completely self-imposed but born out of the experiences we had had along the way. For instance, in the church circles that we moved in, if someone had asked for a prayer for healing and was then not healed, this poor person would come under condemnation and judgement. Thus, after prayer when Simon was not "healed", we felt ourselves judged by others and deemed guilty for some reason beyond our comprehension. We were made to feel that we were the cause of the problem and the blockage to "healing".

It can be really tiresome and annoying to have to experience and deal with ignorant behaviour from other people. This can come in all sorts of shapes and forms and at times when you are least expecting it. We have had plenty of experience over the years including:

- Other children staring, mocking, taunting and then witnessing the children's parents condoning this behaviour or not educating their children about difference, togetherness and acceptance

- Professionals who spent time in our company then professed to know our situation inside out and proceeded to try to fix us (badly)

- Opinions from people about what they would do without anyone taking the time to really listen and find out what we wanted or needed as a family

Consequently, we often felt lonely when we found ourselves in a crowd and we decided to separate ourselves as we did not feel welcome.

Incredibly sociable

Simon is incredibly sociable and will talk to anyone about anything. He really is not shy, but he does not pick up on the social cues given when someone clearly does not want to be bothered; he will just be persistent and persevere with his chat until he gets a response, which is another element of his character that I admire so much.

Other people – the public

During a coach holiday, I remember how some "posh" people were unwilling to chat or get to know us at all. They completely ignored our attempts to talk to them. I am sure this was partly because they did not know how to approach talking to Simon and we presented them with a challenge, causing them to be completely uncomfortable.

Simon has his own unique and wonderful way of communicating in that he speaks using single staccato words, some of which are poorly pronounced. He is a very keen communicator and he wants people to understand him; if he realises that people are struggling to understand him he will begin to spell the word out one letter at a time, but his "d"s, "g"s, "t"s can be very difficult to distinguish. Simon really appreciates it when people write down the letters as he is spelling them out, so he can see if they understand what he means. Alternatively, Simon will go and find some text and point out the word he wants to say within the text; he intently searches and shows great glee when he finds the right word.

Ridiculous suggestions

A number of times in our life we have had to contend with the most ridiculous suggestions. We used to attend a church in Shipley when Simon was about 15. There, we had a good friend called Nora who we had known for some time. However, she once suggested that Simon should go into "a home" as she felt this would be better for us all. This would mean Simon moving out of the family home and into a residential care home for people with learning difficulties. I found her making this suggestion very difficult to stomach. Why would she possibly think it would be better to separate a family who loved each other dearly? I would never suggest such a thing for her family. I would not be so rude or unwise. After this, our friendship dissolved; we couldn't cope with the thought that she felt we would be better off without Simon in our lives. We loved him dearly (and still do and always will). He is our son of whom we are very proud. We are a family unit and we all love each other very much, "a threefold cord is not easily broken!"

We had to face yet another ridiculous suggestion when we first moved into our new home in the 1970s. Some older ladies, who lived down the street, also said that Simon should go into a home. We felt exactly the same as we had the first time! After this we made the choice to have nothing to do with the older ladies again – another friendship lost and afterwards I had the strong inclination to say to them: *'Why don't you go into a home yourself!'* but I never plucked up the courage or strength.

This attitude has continued around us. Even when Simon was 40 years old, a close relative also suggested that Simon should live in a home. Again, we had very little to do with her after that. Why would we want a friendship with someone who felt so little about our son? A few years later she sent an invitation for her daughter's wedding. The invite said to *'Peter and Ann'* and there was no mention of Simon. This was so hurtful and upsetting that I decided to reply saying, *'Peter, Ann and Simon regret that we will be unable to attend.'*

Very offensive

It aggrieves me when people, even church folk and close friends, ask if Simon has "any understanding". This has happened more than you could imagine, even in recent years, and even from people who I thought understood and knew better.

People's comments, including remarks from complete strangers, can be even more offensive. I was once out with Simon, along with a close friend, and we were chatting to each other when a stranger came over to ask, *'is he mentally retarded?'* I was horrified, what a dreadful expression! And a dreadful question! The person didn't show the slightest realisation that they were being rude or offensive or any awareness at all of the impact of what they had asked or how they had made us feel. During these negative interactions and experiences with others it would always amaze me that people did not recognise how rude and ignorant they could be, especially people who talked over the person they are referring to as though they were not there.

Sometimes I think people do not understand the bigger picture or that we are all in this together as a society. They do not see that there are no differences between any of us, just uniqueness. If we could appreciate this, the world would be a much better place.

The cut-off

So, it is true, whenever we experienced negative comments or suggestions, we cut ourselves off from the people who made them, including friends and relatives. We simply couldn't cope with people who thought that way. What could we do to change that? If that's the way people wanted to think — why bother with them?

I realise that I could have spoken to them and encouraged them to be more aware or tried to change their opinion and build their understanding but, in all honesty, I just didn't have the energy, time or interest to have this discussion with them. To do this I would have to muster the energy to respond to them and this sometimes felt like a pointless use of my limited reserves, and therefore things went unsaid, situations went undealt with, and people were left ignorant to the life we were living. I sometimes look back and wish I had said all the things I wanted to say at the time. However, at the time I had to make a decision about whether to use my energy reserves to support my family well or to educate a complete stranger, and both you and I know which decision any parent would make.

I wanted to put my energies into keeping my family together and making the most of every day that we had.

I did, however, find the energy for small responses in the hope that would make a big difference. For instance, whenever a person asked, *'what is wrong with Simon?'* I replied by asking, *'what is right with him?'* or, I would address a question to Simon as the intelligent human being he is, like *'what is the best thing about you?'* Simon would always give a very sound and considered reply.

If life wasn't hard enough just keeping up with day-to-day things, these situations sometimes felt like unnecessary additions to have to deal with.

The most challenging times

As parents we both love Simon dearly; he is our son and we will stand by him and fight for, and alongside, him, for as long as we need to or can.

There are particular times that are difficult for me though. For instance, sometimes in the evenings after a long and hectic day of taking care of

Simon and working with his support workers, doing household tasks, organising appointments, answering numerous phone calls and supporting my lovely husband, Simon can continue to talk incessantly. He can be loud and in need of constant attention; he never stops for breath! At times like these I really have to dig deep to find the energy to support Simon.

In recent years, I have started to find it difficult to cope after 8:30pm. At this time of night Simon can take a long time to settle down, depending on the type of day he has had. He can take up to two and half hours to get ready for and go to bed. By this time my brain has gone to sleep, and it becomes a real slog and a test of my willpower, endurance and faith.

Simon has a number of bedtime routines that are important for him and his health, for example taking care of his ulcers and skin conditions, preparing his skin protection for while he is asleep, which also prevents him from scratching himself during the night, and ensuring his leg protectors are on.

Dog tired

Some nights I have had to apply 13 dressings to sores and this can prove to be very emotionally and physically draining, especially when I am still busy with this at 10:30pm. Simon does not always appreciate why he needs the dressings applying and he can become distracted from the task at hand very easily, which means the biggest job is keeping him focused on the task, and this can be very challenging when you are tired yourself.

Simon is by no means a small man; he is well-built and strong, so physically encouraging him to remain still can be very testing and it adds to the exhaustion and tiredness physically and mentally. In these situations, my faith comes to my rescue.

It is at these times that family carers need ACTION, action fast, something that will quickly alleviate these feelings. It is important for family carers to recognise what helps them during these particularly difficult times and to identify their coping mechanisms. I achieve this through the LOUD singing of worship songs and reading whatever scripture the Lord has given me, for example, psalm 92 verses 12 – 13:

12: 'The righteous will flourish like a palm tree,
they will grow like a cedar of Lebanon;
13: planted in the house of the Lord,
they will flourish in the courts of our God.'

Especially verses 14 and 15:

14: 'They will still bear fruit in old age,
they will stay fresh and green,
15: proclaiming, "The Lord is upright;
He is my rock, and there is no wickedness in him."'

The Bible, Book 4. 92: 12-15

I am then comforted and strengthened by the fact that the Lord knows best and the fears that have been a burden effectively flow away – for me, psalms truly are songs and scriptures of deliverance!

This began one evening when I was feeling a great deal of anguish after a terrible evening with Simon and I said to myself: *'Woman, stop wallowing in grief and self-pity'*. So, I prayed earnestly for the Lord to help me, save me. He immediately gave me worship songs to sing loudly and I was saved from my gloom and self-pity.

'But they that wait upon the Lord
SHALL renew their strength;
They SHALL mount up with wings as eagles;
They SHALL run, and not be weary; and
they SHALL walk, and not faint.'

The Bible, Isaiah. 40:31

Desperation

It's at challenging times like these, such as helping Simon at bedtime, that I feel very close to giving up and, as soon as this feeling starts to rise, all the other associated feelings of guilt, desperation and loneliness begin to seep through. It is the snowball effect; the more tired I become, the worse everything seems to feel, and the more negative feelings start to mount up.

On many occasions I feel extreme desperation, exhaustion and the need to stop and rest but this is not a luxury I have available to me. As a parent I want to love and take care of my son but sometimes I feel I need to be more than one person when looking after him as he requires a lot of extra support, love and attention.

Extreme tiredness

When Simon really plays me up, I start to have feelings of hate towards him. I know how awful and desperate this sounds but I have no energy left to do anything about it.

The only solution I have is to take it to the Lord and rediscover that *'They that wait upon the Lord SHALL renew their strength'* (The Bible, Isaiah. 40:31). I have a Great God, a miracle-working God.

(Knowing that a midnight feast of comfort food is to follow is also uplifting!)

I believe Simon knows when the way he is behaving is exhausting me and pushing me to extremes, but I am sure that, at times, Simon does not know how to change his behaviour – which is equally frustrating for him.

Distancing themselves

It is not uncommon for parents of children with disabilities or mental health issues to sometimes feel like the rest of the world wants to distance itself from them and from caring, particularly when situations like the one where fellow passengers did not want to chat on the coach holiday occur. Suddenly, people who were close friends distance themselves. People at work can become less accommodating to your need to work flexibly; neighbours begin to keep their distance and have less time to chat and people stop calling around.

How people related to us after Simon was born changed significantly. People could not, and would not, see how life was from our perspective and often could not relate to Simon at all.

Distancing myself

Sometimes I had to instigate the distancing in order to be able to cope with my circumstances. A very close friend of mine who I had trained with at St Mary's Hospital, the place where I had trained to be a nurse in London, kept writing to me and telling me about her gorgeous babies and their wonderful achievements. I couldn't bear this as I couldn't write back to talk about my gorgeous baby; life was just too difficult. If I was to write a letter that was truthful it would be full of the problems, feelings of anger and sadness that we faced each day. I stopped writing to her as I couldn't cope; we were living two opposite lives.

The gulf between us

Creating this separation led to greater feelings of isolation and I found that this resulted in a greater pressure to deal with situations without the support networks that we used to have in place. We also missed the invaluable advice that we used to receive from people in our life, people who had experience and a good amount of knowledge.

The emotions of caring

Here are some feelings and strong emotions that I have on a regular basis
– feelings a lot of family carers will be familiar with:

- Guilt
- Despair
- Desolation
- Isolation
- Exhaustion
- Anger
- Resentment
- Grief
- Shame
- Hate
- Suicidal
- Exhilaration
- Protection
- Exaltation
- Pride
- Joy
- Happiness
- Hilarity
- Compassion and
- Overwhelming love.

Often the feelings listed above do not happen in isolation, but they are
cumulative, starting with one challenging emotion and gradually building
into a whole heap of feelings bouncing around and conflicting with each
other. What an emotional conflict! Where do you go from there?!

Family carers can be worn into the ground as a result of all the additional
responsibilities. As a consequence of caring, people do face adversities in
their life like relationship breakdowns, depression, anxiety and divorce.
People who care can, and do, reach a stage of desperation and it has been
known for people to take their own lives and the lives of loved ones. It can
reach awful situations of violence, brutality and murder and this has been
demonstrated in news reports. I have full sympathy with family carers who
find themselves in this position.

Many times, I have reached this level of desperation and I have not wanted to live, but then I come to the realisation that thinking in this way is an unaffordable luxury; my loved ones are dependent upon me – how could I possibly let them down?

It can be a challenge to remain positive and it is during these really testing times that my most negative thoughts have occurred such as:

- *'This is not right!'*
- *'Why can't I do lovely things?'*
- *'I want to get away from all this!'*
- *'I want to run away for good.'*
- *'I want to put an end to all this!'*
- *'It's not fair!'*
- *'I cannot cope!'*

I have had these thoughts on a frequent basis, and I know, from talking to other family carers, that I am not alone; these thoughts are to be expected. These have not just been "passing" thoughts; at times I have thought them through in detail: Where would I go? Who would I go to? What should I do about bank cards? Who would take care of Simon and Peter?

Then, during a calmer time, you have to think it all through and consider the practicalities of it, you have to assess the implications and the devastation you would leave behind if you acted on these thoughts.

These are difficult thoughts to contend with and to manage, especially when you feel so desperate that you feel uncomfortably close to acting on these thoughts. Anyone who finds themselves in a similar situation, experiencing thoughts like these, know that most family carers experience them, so do not feel alone and, most importantly, do not hide them. Feel comfortable talking about them and get them out in the open if possible. Share how you are feeling and find support from others, perhaps by attending a support group to find your direction through them and to find the light at the end of the tunnel. Most importantly I take it to the Lord in prayer and you could do the same if you can.

You are not alone and **do not feel guilty.**

What works for me?

I realised that I needed to find the thing that lifted me up, raised my spirits and enabled me to be confident and to learn to appreciate and love life. For me, Jesus is the key to this: reading psalms and singing hymns loudly (the devil hates that).

The first verse of *"In Christ Alone"* always makes me think *'wow!'* and has helped me on a number of occasions:

'In Christ alone my hope is found,
He is my light, my strength, my song;
This Cornerstone, this solid Ground,
Firm through the fiercest drought and storm.
What heights of love, what depths of peace,
When fears are stilled, when strivings cease!
My Comforter, my All in All,
Here in the love of Christ I stand.'

Getty and Townend, 2012

This is my strength

After I had read the psalms, I had renewed vision and hope, because the psalmist had had the same extreme emotions.

As well as psalms and my faith, I found that appreciating the things that surround us in everyday life, such as the sight of trees and smell of flowers, the smell of baking (and the taste of the finished product of course!), watching the wonderful changing clouds in the sky and the many different shapes and sizes they take on, helped too. All these simple yet effective coping mechanisms still help me today.

Being a parent

Whenever a child is brought into the world it is the start of a whole new journey for the parents. This journey, like any other, has its high points and its low points: wonderful times like when children spread their wings and achieve the unexpected, the fun and embarrassment when a loved one flat out refuses to conform to social norms, and the times when the strength of the child shines through as they prove some people wrong are just some of the highlights.

Being a parent is a lovely, enjoyable and exciting time but it can sometimes bring distress and anguish. This can become more pronounced when you are caring for a child with mental or physical health conditions or learning difficulties, and your role as a parent becomes that of a family carer and a high, intense level of care is likely to be needed over a longer period of time.

A child may be born with health conditions meaning they need extra visits to the hospital and access to specialists, which can be all-consuming. A child with autism will also perceive the world in a completely different way to their parent, which can cause a great deal of confusion, frustration and uncertainty.

Times will get hard and exhausting and you will not know where to find the reserves to deal with the next thing. When this happens, stop for a second and take stock of the delights your child brings to your life every day.

Likewise, life can be surprisingly rewarding for parents, especially when your child's character shines through and they are so loving.

As life goes on and you become an older family carer, it can be unbearable to think about a future life for your child where they will be cared for:

- How will they live and how will they be cared for?
- Will they be safe and happy?
- Will they be turfed out of their home?
- Where will they go?
- What does their future hold?
- What can you tell them?
- How can you reassure them?

Parents hope to be able to bring their child up to be confident and capable to cope with life, but these can be expectations that seem out of reach when your child has learning difficulties, especially when they could be surrounded by people who do not understand them, and they are not able to explain or express their experience. How can you, as a parent, provide reassurance about the future with confidence and integrity?

Making plans for the future can feel impossible because of the uncertainty and the realisation that you have little control when you are not around. Also, when your child, and you as a family, are eligible for support from the health and social care system you realise that this provides little security and certainty for the future, as strategies, law and personnel change so frequently, which makes planning ahead even more daunting.

No better but no worse

In my experience, I have met people who act as though they are superior to people with learning difficulties. I have always found this to be very offensive. We are all equal and NOT ONE OF US is a mistake. We were made in God's image and, as my son points out, *'Jesus was disabled on the cross'*. What we all need to do is recognise all the gifts, skills and talents we all have and learn to appreciate everything we all have to offer.

My son is a fabulous person at prayer and builds the enthusiasm of all the people around when he worships. He is also a brilliant fount of knowledge on all things related to traction engines and is very respected by a lot of members of the traction community. He is actually a fount of information on very many subjects and he often shares his knowledge in passing.

A close and positive relationship

Building a close and positive relationship with your child is vital to enable you to enjoy life to the full. Easy to say, I know(!), but it is possible, as many of the incredible people I know have proved. I can promise you that once you feel your relationship getting closer and stronger you will feel delighted and you will begin to talk about your relationship in a much more positive way.

Do not let the weight of the world stop you from doing the best that you can for your child and, no matter how anyone else views your child and what they think and say, keep loving and doing your best and believing in your child or the person you care for.

What do they know? Why does their opinion matter?! You and your family are the experts.

Tips for a family carer

Developing a positive relationship with your child is one step closer to feeling happier and in more control – once you have conquered this, then you need to think about everyone else. Here are some hints and tips about how we made things better for us:

1. Be proactive – even to the point of being a nuisance; make regular phone calls to the person who provides the answers and/or support you need until you manage to speak to them and get an answer from them. See page 27 for more information on this.

2. Be good at asking and delegating – we have someone who helps us deal with our finances, a lady who is fabulous at decluttering, a lovely person with librarian skills who will sort out all Simon's books and we receive admin support from a lady who can sort through paperwork very efficiently.

3. Networking – make many good contacts. I have lists and lists of the people I have made contact with over the years, from conferences, meetings, appointments and contacts passed to me from other family carers – our address book is very full and well used.

4. Record everything about how your son or daughter wants to be supported or cared for in care plans. These plans could cover the clothes they like to wear, the food they enjoy eating, the people they prefer to spend time with and places they love to go. They could also include the medications they must take, people that can prove useful at times and the routines that are important to them, including health, personal care and the fun stuff.

5. Start a 'circle of support' – a circle of support is wonderful, surrounding yourself with helpful, understanding and uplifting people.

Once you have conquered this then you can think about everything else.

Circle of Support

Simon's circle of support was formed in 2008, after Simon had developed his person centred plan. We thought about the people in our lives who would be the right people to invite to be involved in Simons circle. We could think of a number of people but at first we were concerned about asking them... we had trepidation and we thought that we would be putting on them. We approached them to ask anyway and we received really positive responses with most people stating 'We have always wanted to help'. Everyone close to us would meet up to talk about the current state of Simon's life and how it was going and to make plans for the future. It seemed right to think about a name for Simon's circle meetings and the title "Full Steam Ahead" was adopted.

Simon's circle consisted of Peter and myself, fellow worshippers from his church, people who were paid to support him, his advocate, our financial advisor, other traction engine enthusiasts, some of my colleagues and a neighbour.

Still to this day, "Full Steam Ahead" usually meets up around every three months and this provides a chance to catch up on how things have been going and to make plans for the future. Simon's circle soon became a source of mutual support for one another, offering advice and guidance when needed. The circle members have been incredibly useful when looking at solutions for some of the issues we have faced, including developing a long-term housing plan for Simon, which meant he could remain in the family home, researching events for traction engine enthusiasts and providing encouragement to do new things.

Full Steam Ahead

"Full Steam Ahead" made us realise that we do have some very good friends around even though we have no family and, at times, we can feel lonely. Peter used to always say that we had no friends, but this circle has proved us wrong.

You may find the following template useful to use if you are thinking about setting up your own circle and are considering who to invite to be part of that circle.

Draw four circles on a blank sheet of paper:

Inclusion Europe, n.d.

The inner circle – the people who are very close

In the centre of the circle put the people who are most important and closest to you – this could be your family, friends and loved ones.

The second circle – the people who are very good friends

In the next circle put the people who are friends and individuals that you consider to be good people in your life.

The third circle – the people who are regular acquaintances

In the third circle put the people with whom you are acquainted – this could be people you see during your weekly activities, for instance people you see at church or at the gym.

The fourth circle – the people who are paid to be in our lives

In the last and fourth circle recognise the people who are in your life because they are paid to be there – this could be your GP, support workers and mechanic for example.

How we got started with a Circle of Support

Each family member had a sheet of paper with the circles already on it and each one wrote down their own idea of the people who should be invited to come to our Circle of Support. We discussed these names together and made a list of people we could invite.

I felt very embarrassed about asking anyone to support us but I took courage and took the step to invite the people we had identified. The reactions from my friends were welcoming and encouraging, they all said "Thank you so much I've always wanted to do that".

It was a great relief to know that people I had invited actually want to be involved and to attend our quarterly Circle of Support meetings.

The number of people attending our Circle meetings ranges from ten to fifteen people, but I know of Support Circles that have much fewer members and they are just as effective. We start with pizza and nibbles and then discuss whatever is on the agenda. This tends to be anything that is pertinent and happening in our lives right now, we have discussed things like holidays, health, home and support workers.

A Circle of Support is so precious and special but almost unheard of, especially amongst social workers!

People in the same situation

Up until Simon's twentieth birthday we had not met anyone else who was in the same or similar situation to ourselves. We never saw or met any of the parents of the children that went to school or college with Simon. We had not known that support groups for family carers existed and therefore we hadn't attended any, so we didn't realise that other people faced similar problems to ourselves.

When Simon turned 20, we started to meet parents of children with learning difficulties. At first it was a strange experience to meet people who knew what it was all about, who could understand the difficulties we faced and the challenges we had to tackle. We had never stopped to imagine that other people would be in a similar situation; we had been too focused on taking care of ourselves and avoiding potentially negative experiences.

To avoid the negative comments and prying questions we had chosen to stay away from company and just spend time together in our small family unit. This meant we became a very insular family. For the first time we were meeting other people who just understood. Initially this was strange but, at the same time, reassuring and liberating. We learnt that support groups are good – very good!

I began to appreciate how, when a group of family carers come together, each family is provided with a huge sense of relief. For instance, for us it was the first time we did not feel the need to apologise or explain our situation; everyone was coming from the same place.

When as a family carer I felt isolated, family carers groups I was part of proved to be an invaluable lifesaver.

Family carers really do need all the help they can get.

Day Care

The first family carers group I joined was at a Day Care Centre. There were many family carers who joined this group and one family carer in particular was very vocal about changing how things were for people with learning difficulties and their family carers. I did admire her passion, although there were times when this became a bit of a pain and quite draining; she complained a lot and did not get anywhere very fast. Often all the other family carers wanted was just a little time out, a place to chat and relax, a bit of peace and some action to improve their situation.

I remember Simon joining a youth club that had been specifically set up for young people with learning difficulties. The club ran on an evening. The mother of Maureen, a good friend of Simon's, was a prominent organiser of the club. We all went to this group together and it was the first social group Peter joined.

Finally, Peter had a chance to make friends that he still has now. This was a wonderful experience for Peter and this group supported him to feel more secure and less isolated. It was a well organised group and they had a lot going on; it was a busy and active place. Simon had the chance to have a go on a computer for the first time and it was there where he learnt how to type. This became an important pastime for Simon as he made use of the computer to communicate stories with others and write what he called his "rumours", short stories that he had written that were either completely fictional or, at times, based on fact. Simon could serve a real swerve ball by mixing fact with fiction, which could cause some very amusing confusion.

Family carers coming together

Meeting up with other family carers was such a relief for me, and led to unexpected friendships based on compassion, respect, understanding and a mutual offer of support.

It was in 1985 when I first became connected to a family carers group, which seems like a very long time ago. Since then, I have had a constant source of support, fun and understanding. I believe I have also been gifted with the opportunity to provide support to other family carers. Through making these connections and striking up these friendships, I have learnt that I can be comfortable in our situation and that how we lived wasn't that unusual after all; we no longer needed to hide or be insular.

I continue to feel awkward and uncomfortable in other groups or social situations, whether this is a class, a choir, or a social group. When people ask the question, "what do you do?" I begin to explain that I am a family carer and I start to give an insight into our family life, which can often be a conversation killer. Being a family carer can be too much for people to comprehend and too much to explain.

Sharing the Challenge – a unique course for family carers

In 2008, I attended a course called "Sharing the Challenge", which turned out to be the answer to many prayers for countless family carers, especially mine.

This intensive short course ran in my local area and was developed by Partners in Policymaking, a free scheme that taught carers and their families the power advocacy could have to positively change lives. It was geared to be delivered at times that would be feasible for family carers to attend. It ran for two days every fortnight and each day started at 10am and finished at 3pm. This made it much easier to fit around other caring responsibilities. "Sharing the Challenge" was an innovative programme for parents of children and adults with learning difficulties. It was designed to educate and empower its participants, so they could achieve positive change in their own life and that of their family as well as at local and national levels.

Whilst on the course, we had the opportunity to develop an understanding of our collective experiences, building strength by sharing stories. We learnt about the history of learning disability provision, the perception of disability and our rights underpinned by law.

This course was delivered by a fun and inspiring mum indeed, Lynne Elwell, who, herself had been through many trials, tribulations and sadness; she had been through the mill. Her openness and positive attitude were infectious. We all knew she understood as she had been there before. Lynne has written a very useful book to support family carers. This is referenced at the end of this book (Elwell, 2018).

Attending this course changed my life and, as a result, I became a proactive family carer with a strong vision and an understanding of our rights.

Everyone who attended gained encouragement, strength, a clear vision and direction. I left the course confident in the knowledge I had acquired, bold and surrounded by useful contacts. I felt inspired and realised that my actions could make a difference.

Contacting our local MP

The following summer I made appeals to the local authority via an MP after visiting their surgery, to gain assurance over Simon's future and the support he would receive. It was clear from past experiences of services that Simon had previously received that he could not live in a shared living scenario where he had to live with a large group of people. Our greatest fear was Simon being taken away by the local authority, a fear of social services shared by all family carers.

When we spoke to Simon about his living arrangements and options, he made it very clear that he wanted to continue to live at home. He was very anxious to know that he could, and we wanted to help make this possible. Together with Simon's fabulous advocate, an IMCA (independent mental capacity advocate), we approached our local MP to raise their awareness and ask for their input. This led to the MP investigating matters and we gained the assurances we were looking for. What a result!

More concerns

Again in 2008 we had concerns about the level of care and support Simon was receiving. Once more we contacted our local MP to make them aware of the desperation we were experiencing with regard to the local authority. We received good replies, like the one below, illustrating that it really is worth writing to MPs.

Dear Ms Brown

Thank you very much for your recent correspondence, the contents of which I have fully taken on board.

I have today written immediately to the council on your behalf and I will be in touch with you again as soon as I receive a response to the representations I have made.

In the meantime, if I can be of assistance to you or if you wish to let me know your views on any other issue, please do not hesitate to contact me.

Yours sincerely

MP

Receiving support of this type provided us with confidence and renewed energy to fight for the support Simon needed at a time when we otherwise felt ignored, overruled and desperate.

Campaigns

In the same year I joined 50 family carers who were appealing against the local authority and health board regarding a young lady who had been detained wrongly, illegally. She had been incarcerated, misdiagnosed and receiving the wrong treatment at Wenfield Mount, a high security assessment and treatment unit in Bradford. We all campaigned and wrote to local MPs, the social care and health commissioners, everyone "except the Pope". In the end, we went to the press, who published her story, so she was eventually released after six months of incarceration and bad treatment. Now she has a fabulous life; she lives in her own accommodation and has paid support workers who come to work with her and know her well. She goes out to parties and is supported to do the things she wants to do, which includes enjoying life to the fullest and looking beautiful.

Another issue I appealed against was the "yellow card". This card was introduced for people in receipt of social care support as a way for them to pay for their cash contribution towards their social care provision. At the time, social services were requesting a lot of money from Simon for his contribution towards the cost of his care and transport. When Simon was making these contributions, it was a financially difficult time for us; we were much stretched, and we had no surplus available to cover these contributions. As part of the appeal, we proved that we spent more on Simon than he received in benefits, as is the case for most family carers. It often goes unrecognised that the cost of living with a learning difficulty, or any disability, is much higher than your average cost of living. This is considering all the supplements, equipment and therapies that are needed and the higher utility bills due to having to wash clothes and bedding more often and to maintain a certain temperature in the home, as well as general household wear and tear, all costs which are often not taken into account.

Again in 2000, I wrote an appeal, this time about the carer's allowance. Unfortunately, my appeal was unsuccessful this time. I had just retired, and the carer's allowance stops at the age of 60 when you get your pension, irrelevant of whether you are still a family carer. I found then, and still do find this unfair for older people who are still caring for someone in their family.

Grants

In 2004 and 2005 I applied for a carer's holiday grant to enable a group of family carers to go on a group holiday to Italy with the people they cared for. Some people needed financial support to be able to attend and we needed the grant to cover their costs. We were successful! The holiday happened and people had a great time, creating many fond and lasting memories, further strengthening the relationships and the support we could offer one another.

I also applied 2006 for a carer's grant, which is available for anyone who fulfils a caring role and who could utilise the grant for something that would significantly change their life for the better. Therefore, I was eligible, and I decided to apply to get some funding for a pond for our little garden; I love ponds and the wildlife that they attract. With delight I was successful, and my application was approved. The pond reminds me of some wonderful childhood memories and is a source of much needed relaxation. It is positioned so I can sit and watch from both inside and outside the house. I like to watch the frogs cavorting, the spring birds bathing and the dragonflies. I also admire the marsh marigolds and gorgeous rushes. Praise God for this – a great source of pleasure and delight!

A proactive and productive phone call

During this period of my life I also learnt how to make a phone call as a proactive person to someone who was really not interested and did not want to help. Here is the "10 point plan" strategy I developed and the steps I would take each time I needed to make a call:

1. Write out your case beforehand so you have all the points in front of you.

2. Get the person you need to speak to on the telephone.

3. Note down the name of the person you are speaking to.

4. Record the date and time you are speaking to them, so you have a record of the conversation.

5. Let them know you are recording the conversation and the reason you are phoning them.

6. Write down the name of their boss.

7. Lay it on very thick and include every detail of your plight. Keep on talking and don't let them go.

8. When they say they will phone you back, ask "when?" Pin them down.

9. If they say, for example, "this afternoon", say "when?"

10. If they say, for example, "by 3pm", say "if you haven't rung by 2:55pm I will phone you." Then they know that they must take you seriously.

I would keep an accurate record of all conservations until the matter had been dealt with. This approach had a good success rate and I found I was able to get things addressed and dealt with much quicker this way.

Losing support

For a long period of time I was greatly helped by a carer's support worker called Maddy, but, in 2009, the national organisation who employed her made redundancies and we lost her role, despite the fact that, for the previous seven years, she had made a very big difference in the lives of many family carers.

A group of proactive family carers, including myself, contacted our local MPs and the press to raise awareness regarding how local family carers were losing a vital source of support. Although we campaigned, the decision was not reversed – you can't win them all! The last meeting with Maddy had about seventy-five family carers present; it was a heartfelt occasion with despair, grief and anger. From that point onwards, there would be at least seventy-five family carers and families in Bradford desperately trying to get by without the support they needed.

To this day I still feel it is a desperate situation that there is not enough support for family carers and so many family carers are left to flounder in the dark, clutching around in despair, feeling all these emotions. People who are family carers need good support and they deserve it.

A family carer's health

We have to be aware of how the caring role affects the health and wellbeing of the family carer, as I know all too well from my own experiences of ill health. Family carers have a very high level of responsibility and are always on the go. It's easy for family carers to ignore indicators that their own health is failing as they feel the need to carry on. When a family carer feels that their own health is in danger often a huge sense of panic can follow, and they can find themselves asking: "Who will take care of my loved ones if I can't?!"

"Look after yourself"

"Look after yourself". I know people mean well when they say this, but I find it very annoying. I believe it shows a great lack of understanding. How is it possible for you to look after yourself when you need to spend all your time looking after someone else or other people? When I hear someone say this it feels like they do not want to recognise how they could possibly help take care of the family carer they are addressing or give them a break. It feels like a closing statement and the end of a conversation. They don't want to hear anymore, and it lacks integrity. Maybe, if they really meant what they said, they should help somehow? Instead, ask the family carer, "how can I help?" or "what can I do to help to take something off your plate?"

Not every family carer has the same feelings that I do towards the phrase "look after yourself". One family carer once told me that it was the very best advice they had been given by a fellow family carer at a time when she was caring for her son, her mum and a child she was fostering through social services. *'Had this other family carer not been so intense and insistent that I act upon her advice I really would have been physically, mentally, emotionally and spiritually depleted.'* (Thompson, 2018a). For some family carers, it is hard to recognise the need to take care of their own wellbeing and it therefore takes someone with an outside perspective to tell them what's best for them.

Experiencing ill health

After we had moved to Allerton in 1967, I developed a horrendous continuous headache. It was excruciating and left me in a state where I was unable to do anything. This became so bad that I was eventually rushed into Bradford Royal Infirmary. While I was there, the doctors assessed me and I was put onto a side ward to undergo lumbar punctures and observation.

Maybe it was a "one-off" enormous migraine, but I thought I had encephalitis, which is inflammation and swelling of the brain. The symptoms became worse every time I laid down, which meant it was impossible for me to get the rest and sleep I needed. This was a very difficult time for me, and I found the illness hard to cope with. I had to be away from home and my family, and I was concerned about whether Peter and Simon were okay without me. Peter and I worried that I wouldn't make a full recovery and were concerned about how we would keep the family together if that was the case. Encephalitis is quite a dangerous condition, so we were all concerned. Although I never received an official diagnosis, the symptoms I had matched those of the condition. Many people were praying for me and for us.

Praise God, within a week I had recovered enough to be able to come home. Whilst I was in hospital, a family friend named Emily took care of Simon and Peter. Afterwards, Emily reported that she found it very challenging to take care of Simon and to keep him occupied and entertained; even in that week she had become quite exhausted. I think Emily was the only person who ever got involved with our family to such an extent as to really appreciate how difficult and challenging it could be and how much energy and strength it took to keep everything going.

What I cannot do

As an older parent who is taking care of an adult son and husband there are a number of things I cannot do. These include:

- Having an early night.
- Going away for the day.
- Having a day off when I please.
- Keeping in touch with family and friends.
- Having romantic time with my husband.
- Keeping the house as I would like (it tends to be chaos!)
- Learning new things like MP3 players and computers.
- Reading the books or watching the films I would like to see.
- Attending courses to pursue interests.

All these things are important to me, but I am not able to do any of them.

I would love to become IT literate as it would enable me to use Skype correctly to keep in touch with my sisters in America and Australia. When we attempt a connection, we blunder through with varying results – sometimes we can hear each other but cannot see each other and sometimes we can see each other but cannot hear a thing. I would also like to be able to write this book easily using a computer, so I am able to see everything on a screen!

What I would love

I would love to have a hospitable, open house like the one we had when we first married and like the one my sister, Katie, has now in Australia. It would be great to be able to open my home to anyone, help the homeless, lay on food and refreshments and have friends visit.

I would like to have a house full of glorious house plants of different shades and scents. My grandmother, mother and sisters all had green fingers.

I do not have the time or the talent for garden plants. However, over the years houseplants often crept into the house.

I nurtured and cherished them as best I could. If a plant had an ailment, I would study the cause and nurse it back to health. This took so much time and I had varying results. Twice in my life I have had to have a good clear-out of all the houseplants. I got rid of them all; I simply could not spare the time for them.

I would love to be able to travel and explore anywhere intrepidly – it's in my genes.

I wish I could spend more time enjoying fabric and material shops, to drool over the beautiful materials on offer and maybe have the time/ability to make wonderful clothes. When Simon was young, I had more time so, in the evenings, I used to make all our clothes. We rarely shopped for new clothes, and never used charity shops. I made many great clothes, from a warm overcoat for Simon to all Peter's trousers. I couldn't quite make everything though and still haven't quite progressed into men's tailored jackets.

I love the clouds in a blue sky, but I rarely have time to venture into the country or even go out for a walk. However, I do go into the attic to sit and enjoy the clouds in the sky through the Velux windows. This is a real treat. Also, large supermarket car parks are great for seeing a range of wondrous clouds and a large sky – I love them! Thank you, Jesus, for your beautiful, mysterious and majestic skies that are continually repainted!

I would like to have more time to read, go to art groups, play bowls, go to singing workshops and be more involved at church.

I would also appreciate being able to get on top of the paperwork and finances without panicking about it and having the time to declutter and blitz the house.

I love to hear of the wonderful things that others have done, fabulous walks, lovely places visited, but it hurts slightly that I am unable to do it, or that they didn't think that I might like to join them.

Being aware we are not an island – we must acknowledge our responsibilities

Sometimes we do not even realise how difficult people are finding it to cope with life's day-to-day demands, even for people who are only taking care of themselves.

A friend of mine once went to a man's funeral, and afterwards she went to help his brother clear the house. The brother was utterly shocked at the state of the house; it was in a complete mess, chaotic, and very unhygienic with no gas, water or electricity. He always imagined his brother lived well as he had always been so well turned out. He was the picture of a gracious well-kept gentleman, but his home told a completely different story. It transpired that he never, ever ate at home, he didn't heat it and it had all begun to decline when his wife left him.

So, we do have a bigger responsibility for our spouses and each other than we may realise. We cannot just ignore situations when our loved ones are finding it a challenge to cope. We need to support and be there for one another as much as we can. It would be too selfish and short-sighted to not support each other. This was an eye opener for me as I realised that, at times, I also felt like walking out, but this was the very reason why I couldn't.

Sharing your caring experiences can have surprising effects...

As a family carer it can be very difficult to be open with others about your personal life but if you can find the strength to share your story someone will be helped by hearing it. They may think: "you have just described my life". This could then be an untold source of support for that person. The realisation that they are not the only person experiencing difficulties and that other people around them are going through the same issues can reduce a person's feelings of isolation and loneliness.

Family carers dealing with officialdom

It was especially difficult for us as a family, as it is for all family carers, when we finally decided to reach out and ask for help from the services available and the local authority. Instead of a source of support, we found that we had in fact just engaged in another battle. All our fears of approaching the local authority for support were realised. The people from the local authority got involved in our lives, but they didn't listen. Instead, they expected us to listen to them and then they told us what we should do and how we needed to change. The last thing we expected was to have to justify ourselves and to take on another battle where we felt questioned, judged and at the behest of another person's opinion, but this is exactly what we experienced.

It is not uncommon for family carers and families to feel ostracised and not listened to when professionals get involved in their lives, especially when professionals are engaging with them for the first time. A friend of mine experienced similar feelings when it came to caring for her foster son, Keith, which she recounts below. Steph's experience makes me realise that I am not alone.

> 'I was a long-term link worker for Keith*, employed as a paid (expenses!)/voluntary carer (at 62.5p per hour) for over ten years.

> 'As a single parent caring for my small son, poorly mother and aunt (bipolar) and holding down a 30-hour job, I received little support from social services or the council.

> 'I became overwhelmed by paperwork, accounts, doctors and hospital appointments, day centre meetings, social services meetings/visits, telephone calls, faxing, writing letters and the like; I became exhausted. I was quickly drowning with all the expectations – they could see this but kept stating:

'"It's about Keith and his needs must come first."

'"You can't treat Keith like a member of the family!"

'"You can't correct Keith's bad behaviour!"

'"You can't restrain Keith if he hits out/becomes violent!"

'The list is endless.

'Friendships and relationships faded, family visited less, invites dried up (how many times can you turn friends/family down because you only have 20 days respite and no sitting service (this was personal time for me)?)

'I was becoming more isolated and housebound by the day (work and meetings became a blur!) My mental health started to suffer, and I began "counselling". When Keith found out, he refused to go to his day centre and, as I couldn't leave him alone or with anyone else, I had to take him along with me! What use of counselling was that? (He used to use it against me! He would sleep at the centre and have me up all night...)

'All this time social services knew my plight and chose to turn a "blind eye". They never really offered any genuine support; it either benefitted Keith or "them"! They barked out the orders and demands.

'I was breaking under the pressure. Keith became increasingly jealous of my son and started to become violent towards him and his friends and towards my family and friends when they visited (my son was growing up and no longer the "kiddy").

'It took social services over a year to find a suitable residence for Keith (after I insisted on it being a safe placement for all concerned).

'The whole experience left me isolated, exhausted, lacking confidence and phone phobic'.

'It was not the real world at all, but a world they created.'

Thompson, 2018b

It is vital that parents, family carers and families are recognised for the knowledge and understanding they have for the person they care for as they, themselves deserve respect for the care and support they have provided over the years and what they have learnt about each other in this time. **They are the experts.**

How can "they" judge?

From an outside perspective life may not be perfect in the family home but what is perfect? Is anything perfect all the time? It also has to be recognised and assumed that the family have done the very best they can and that they may have been working and getting by under very difficult circumstances, such as:

- Having a limited income.
- Having limited time to meet all their family commitments and responsibilities.
- Trying to meet all the demands whilst exhausted and potentially contending with health problems, both physical and mental, due to caring.
- Having a reduced support network.

It is also important that professionals do not assume or judge people against their own expectations about what constitutes a good quality of life, in terms of the type of houses people live in, the make of cars people drive or their daily routines.

I have learnt that family carers have to fight hard persistently for their rights in most aspects of their life but especially with the local authorities; and this becomes another source of stress, anxiety and exhaustion.

When we were first in contact with the local authorities, we felt that the people we were put in contact with were "sitting in their throne rooms" casting opinions, telling us what we had to do, what we couldn't do and what we could have, when all we needed was to be respected as intelligent and capable people who needed a bit of support.

Just listen to us!

Rather than the professionals listening to our story, hearing what we were struggling with and helping us to find solutions to overcome our challenges, they told us what service we could have, irrelevant of whether this was helpful. Most of the professionals who have intervened over the years have had no personal experience of caring – how could they possibly understand?

Family carers are already exhausted and at the end of their tether; the last thing that is needed is to have to fight against the system. But we more often than not find the strength to take on this fight.

This comes in all shapes and sizes and from all directions. Challenges we encountered included getting past a receptionist to speak to the right people (the receptionists are the first "gatekeepers") and changing our routines or how we were with one another to meet expectations of professionals, all of which we had already attempted and it had failed but they had not taken the time to find this out or learn about us.

What family carers need

When a family carer reaches out for help, what they really need is for someone to listen and to respond to their situation, which can be desperate, and to help make things better, not worse.

Some advice for professionals

Anyone reading this story who fulfils a paid role in someone's life, whether you are a social worker, support worker, nurse or receptionist, remember you are in the privileged position to be paid to make a positive difference in people's lives.

Family carers are very remarkable people due to what they achieve; their strength, resilience and the interesting things they have done and continue to do. They are to be admired as the source of knowledge and expertise that they are, but instead many feel that they are worthless, that they have to justify themselves and that they are judged on a very regular basis.

I hope these quotes from caring events I have attended illustrate how to support family carers:

How to help family carers

- *'Listen.'*
- *'Be understanding.'*
- *'Understand that this is not the life we would have chosen.'*
- *'We're given this life and want to do our best in it.'*
- *'Help us in the fight (struggle) against official and petty obstacles.'*
- *'Appreciate carers and realise that they are a valuable resource.'*
- *'Be honest about services – don't defend the system.'*
- *'As someone in a paid role it is important to listen to the people you are paid to support, recognise them as capable people that are the experts in their own life. You are working with people who have reached a stage in their lives where they need support to continue to function and contribute to their communities.'*
- *'Listen to people, learn from them and respect them for who they are.'*

Heroes

A family carer's sense of self-worth can be low, and they may not feel valued by the world. When first meeting a family carer, who may appear defensive and tired, be aware of the experiences they have been through, and the reasons they feel this way.

Family carers are incredibly important and valuable, not only to their own families but to the rest of society; they are incredible people and they are heroes.

Insight from a support worker

A support worker who had worked with Simon for a number of years demonstrated a real insight into our lives as family carers and how some of the day-to-day tasks that can be taken for granted in other people's lives can be incredibly difficult for the person who is cared for and the family.

'Cooking a meal – this can be dangerous at times as it can involve moving around with hot items, drinks etc.

'Simon tends not to be very dextrous and breakages occur on a regular basis. A piece of "Capodimonte" will likely be handled in the same manner as an old mug.

'Being "careful" is often not a priority for Simon and TVs, DVDs, computers, books, etc. suffer mortal damage.

'Sleep can be constantly disrupted. When Simon gets up at 3:30am then someone else has to for obvious safety reasons.

'Simple journeys can be traumatic and, although Simon loves using public transport, he would find this impossible without support with him.

'Simon has autism. Walking from one kind of surface to another e.g. stairs or carpet to wooden floor can be a nightmare for him as this feels very scary and dangerous to him. Simon's spatial awareness is affected by his autism.

'Eating out in cafes, pubs, restaurants – Simon eats faster and less "tidily" than the rest of us and tends to be pointed at and moved away from in such venues. Some people will even complain.

'Family emergencies – Simon's family carers cannot just drop everything to help someone else as most people can. Everyday things can be problematic to a family with a member who has a learning difficulty.

'It can be difficult to stop and chat with friends, neighbours or acquaintances at a bus stop or in a shop or supermarket. Sometimes people think you're rude or stand-offish.

'It can be difficult to have a telephone conversation due to Simon causing a distraction and making a lot of noise, or simply because he just needs our full attention.

'Routines and disruptions at home make it almost impossible to have friends round.'

Kirkham, 2011

To social workers and professionals

I can only hope that people choose to enter this type of work for the right reasons: because they want to be caring and compassionate and have a desire to help people and improve their situation, knowing that, with the right tools, they can help people in distress. I encourage people to never lose sight of this and, no matter how difficult and challenging it can be, to find a way to meet the aspirations and outcomes wanted by the person and their family, whilst also meeting the requirements of the professional caring role and the regulations of professional caring work – strict regulations and protocols that paid carers must work within.

When this challenge becomes overwhelming and the way forward is difficult to identify, take a step back and re-focus on the person as they must be the priority when making decisions about what step to take to help make their life better, not worse.

Family carers and service improvement

It is not an uncommon situation for family carers to give their time, which is very precious and in high demand, to work alongside professionals to improve what is available through local service structures. I have known family carers to be actively involved in consultations about improving or changing service delivery in adult social care, health and education. At the end of the process and consultations, family carers often feel completely overlooked and their contributions ignored. It often seems that the outcomes have already been predetermined by the senior managers, and that the consultations simply exist to serve as evidence that they have taken place to placate family carers and keep them quiet. Family carers are proactive, they campaign, and they go to their local MPs and to the Houses of Parliament with a mission to improve the life experiences of their children and others in the same situation. Service providers, commissioners and senior managers need to be aware that family carers have a great deal of insight and knowledge to share, they have brilliant ideas and practical solutions to longstanding problems and, most importantly, they are extremely resourceful. Family carers are the **experts** and worthy of great respect.

A higher profile for family carers

Family carers have, over the years, started to receive a higher profile, with reports and research conducted about the impact of caring and the level of commitment required to care. A report published by Mencap (2006) called *"Breaking Point"* really highlighted the challenges and inequalities faced by family carers. However, there is still a low level of attention given to family carers regarding listening to them, acting upon their views and ensuring that they feel cared for themselves. There are a lot of nice things said, but not a lot of action or support that makes a real difference. Nothing much changes! "We've been there before."

One size fits all

Since we first asked for help from our local authority, we have been offered a number of service solutions; there wasn't a great deal of choice and we were told what Simon could have in a fashion of "that or nothing". These services did not work for Simon, in fact they caused a great deal of distress for him and our family. Simon has attended a respite service and a day service – none of which worked for him and he became distressed in these places. This was partly because they were understaffed. They would have one person working with a room full of twenty-two people; they had no training in autism or in Simon's particular problems; other people there would bully him or tell him off if they did not like what he was doing, despite bad behaviour very often being a cry for help.

He then became known throughout the service as being challenging and a difficult person to support when, in fact the reason he was behaving in that way was because he had been overpowered, ignored and told what to do as nobody listened to him. The irony!

Professionals unable to think outside the box

Before he attended these places, we did share our thoughts about how they would not work for him with professionals and how we knew how Simon would respond. They were not interested in what we had to say, and they were not trained to think outside the box; they could only refer to what was available and sadly, did not have the creativity, freedom or time to think about what could be possible.

How a personal budget became our lifeboat

It was really clear that no service would work for Simon, so, after a very long time spent trying, we were offered a different solution, at first a direct payment and now we currently receive a personal budget. This means that Simon is now supported in a way that works well for him. He has a small team of dedicated workers who support him in a positive and respectful way. They have a mutually respectful relationship and share similar interests and senses of humour. Simon can choose where he goes and what he does, and he doesn't feel trapped in one place. He is happy, and it works better for the whole family; we feel much more in control. I feel as though I have a bigger and safer family, while his paid carers feel as though they have got "their lives back again".

Simon has the freedom to do the things that he enjoys each day, such as going to museums, visiting different towns and cities, going on bus rides and shopping for "bothers" and books ("bothers" are items he finds in charity shops that spark his interest).

For this to work well, it is important that Simon receives support from people that value him. The team that supports Simon believe that people have the right to lead their own lives in a way that makes sense to them, to be a part of their local community, to be included, to contribute and to be respected.

From Simon's former support workers – what does it mean to be a support worker?

Some of Simon's support workers wrote about what it means to them to be a support worker:

- *'I love to see the people I support happy and enjoying themselves.'*
- *'I think it is important for the people I support to have the opportunity to go out and about in their local community and experience different things which they are interested in.'*
- *'I enjoy supporting people with a wide range of abilities/disabilities. Overall, I feel very rewarded to be in the job I am in.'*
- *'Here are the things I think are important:*
    - o *Giving something back to the community.*
    - o *Helping improve the quality of someone's life by sharing experiences, knowledge and enabling the person.*
    - o *Having a laugh and joke – banter.*
    - o *Focusing on the person, not the disability.*
    - o *Reward of a job well done, more than money/financial reward.*
    - o *Being trusted by the person you support or care for.*
    - o *Learning not be judgemental and accepting the person and each other for who they/we are.*
    - o *Treating the person as an equal.*

Simon's world

Simon's person centred planning facilitator stated that it would be a good idea to have all the information that I held about how to care for and support Simon written down in one document. We have compiled a very full, fat folder that captures everything you need to know to support Simon well. We have called this document *"Simon's World"* and it is detailed and thorough documentation that covers everything from daily routines, favourite places to go and his own particular language – so we all know how to communicate well – to a list of publications that Simon likes to read, information about his circle of support and key phone numbers and contacts. *Simon's World* is a very, very useful resource to assist anyone supporting Simon in getting to know him well. Writing this documentation has given me the confidence and reassurance that I have imparted all the knowledge and love I have for my son.

A burden lifted

Before writing *Simon's World*, I felt a huge burden that only I knew this information about Simon and worried about what would happen if I wasn't around, so I committed myself to documenting it all and it took a very long time. So much information had been rattling around my head, no wonder I was tired! My hope is that everything I know and understand about Simon is now written down for other people to provide the same level of support, care and understanding that we have provided him with over the years when we are no longer able to do so.

Insight from a student social worker

A student social worker helped me review *Simon's World*. She also spent time with a family carers group called Bradford Plan, which supported its members – who were made up of family carers – to achieve a good life for the people they cared for, ensuring they were part of and enjoyed everyday life, as well as being an active and important part of their communities. She listened to other family carers' accounts of their experiences, both good and bad, and had a chance to gain an insight into my life as a family carer and into the lives of other family carers. This is an excerpt from the student social worker's report that she completed as part of her placement coursework:

> ### How my view on family carers has changed as a student social worker over the past two years
>
> *'I began my social work course two years ago and my view on family carers back then was that they were people who simply cared for their family and made sure that their needs were met.*

'Now, after working with Ann, Peter and Simon and other family carers, I have come to the conclusion that family carers are so much more than somebody looking after their loved one. I have realised that for a family carer there are no holidays and no weekends off; being a family carer is a 24/7 job. Even when the person being cared for is asleep or away, the family carer is still working to ensure that everything is ready for their loved one. The family carer's job is to ensure that the benefits they are entitled to are applied for and that other people working with their loved one are capable of meeting the needs of their loved one. The family carer has to ensure medicine is administered correctly and that any appointments their loved one needs to attend are made and then attended.

'A full-time family carer spends all of their life worrying about their loved one, making plans for what will happen in unforeseen circumstances and ensuring finances are accessible for their loved one should anything happen to the family carer. Without their family carer the loved one's life would be extremely difficult. There is not a lot of recognition for family carers, especially family carers who are looking after elderly or adult family members. When family carers are spoken about in the media, mainly family carers of young children are discussed.

'Whilst working with Ann I have realised that in the days her son was growing up there was little support for family carers and people believed that people who were seen as having a disability belonged in an institution. Not only has Ann faced being a family carer for the past 50+ years, she has managed to do this whilst working and providing for her family. She ignored the prejudices she experienced and faced life with a smile on her face.

'Overall, my view of family carers now is that they are people who have the weight of the world on their shoulders, but they do what they do out of enjoyment as well as out of love for the person they are caring for. Their job is a hard job that *involves a lot of physical tasks as well as the effect it has on the family carer's emotional state. Unlike a professional job where you are able to try and distance yourself from your clients, a full-time family carer does not have this luxury. They are responsible for the wellbeing of their loved one. This entails ensuring that they are eating the correct food, getting enough rest and taking the correct medications. The family carer also has to ensure that their loved one is being provided with activities to keep them active and healthy.*

'From what I can see after spending time with Ann, a family carer's job is a hard job but a rewarding job.'

Anon., 2014a

From the horse's mouth – nuggets of insight from other family carers

What do family carers think?

Here are some contributions from family carers who were members of Bradford Plan. In these snippets of information people have shared what it has been like to be a family carer – the good, the bad and the ugly:

'It has been difficult to use public transport as he is unsteady on his feet. On the bus he is always grabbing to help feel steady, but this can make for problems if he grabs someone by accident or if he grabs past someone to hold onto a bar.'

'Phone conversations can be difficult, and friends don't always understand why.'

'Even with church visitors I feel nervous.'

'I feel folk are pathetic, for not showing understanding or empathy for their fellow citizens.'

'We as a family have grown up with them [the person they care for], we have learnt as we have gone along. Our generation had to get along and cope.'

'They [the professionals] thought it was "my problem." I had to go and find what we needed and find a way to get by.'

'I overheard someone say, "It is a shame, they should have been put down at birth."'

'It is annoying when something is advertised as "accessible", and it is not so.'

'We had an ordinary buggy; no-one told us of the facilities/equipment that were available. It was awkward for us to use. I realise looking back that we hadn't heard of a lot of things.'

'Some people just think of them as being a very naughty child.'

'Before I was a mum, I went to work at Northwood Hospital. This was a hospital for people with learning disabilities. A lot of people lived there [but it has since been shut]. Before starting the job, I was nervous about spending time with people with disabilities. On my first day I said to myself, "Why am I coming here? I am frightened!" but I got to know people and learnt that they are just the same as everyone else.'

'She was so hyperactive that staff at the respite unit where she stayed said that they couldn't cope. So, we were left with the option of her being at home all the time, with no break away from full-time care.'

'She used to get lost and all the kids were looking for her.'

'Hospitals are a nightmare, she runs away from "white coats"' [this goes back to the days when people were often in a hospital setting].

'Staff can be really lovely.'

'Her care staff all have different attributes, but it usually works.'

'When she needs a filling, she needs an anaesthetic.'

'Sometimes I just can't cope.'

'He needed a speech therapist, but the therapist that came was clueless. I kept pushing for another speech therapist, until someone marvellous came. She got on the floor with him, lying down. That worked! It is no good sitting at a desk and looking important.'

[About her daughter taking part in a cheerleading competition.] 'All the able-bodied competitors accepted those with disabilities and cheered them and cheered them, there was no issue.'

'Whilst travelling on a train one young lady was very difficult, so I said audibly to my disabled son, "Leave her alone, she can't cope."'

'We all said this could happen to anyone, this could happen to any of us.'

'She has been going to football for over 30 years and has never had a problem. She likes the rowdy atmosphere.'

'Pantomimes are OK because they are a bit rowdy.'

'She gets agitated in crowds, especially strangers, and a baby crying distresses her because as a baby she was left to cry at the end of a yard.' [by her birth parents – quote here is given by the adoptive family].

'Once we took him to Shakespeare's The Taming of the Shrew, as he knew the star of the show, an actor called Richard. They got on well; Richard told him all about the play and took him backstage. My son behaved wonderfully and even laughed at some jokes that other people missed. Another time we took him to a band concert and we didn't prepare for it at all; he behaved really badly, and I could have hidden under the chair!'

'Went to a wedding once and she went around all the glasses and took a sip out of each one. We laughed but it was traumatic.'

'Mum is really exhausted, and she floats in and out of sleep,

196

which is brought on by being the main supporter/carer. She is in her late '70s.'

'What we have done, we have done with the best intentions. We are all worried that we have done the right thing.'

'The educational professional was convinced that she should go to nursery, against our better judgement. It lasted three weeks!'

'We have been through the mill.'

'Marriages can fail, because of the strain of having to take second place.'

'We haven't really had a holiday; Mum couldn't cope.'

'Some people are on a different planet; they don't really know about life.'

'What makes me cross are comments like, "Oh you are wonderful!", "I couldn't do that!", "You were born for it" and "You are in for a special place in heaven." Those comments are really annoying.'

Anon., 2014b

A story from another family I know well

Here is a detailed insight into what life is like when you have a son with a learning disability, contributed by another family carer:

'When Lee was born with Down's syndrome, family and friends felt very sorry for me, but this changed when they saw how positive and happy I was to have him. His dad struggled with his disability and found it difficult to tell people about him. Public reaction has always been mixed; some people are friendly towards him, others distant, wary of his disability.

'As a child, Lee didn't like walking very far, and when he'd had enough he would just sit down on the pavement and refuse to move, even if I walked off a little way from him. (Reactions from the public to this were interesting and sometimes a little annoying when he would do something for a complete stranger that he wouldn't do for me!) However, taking a steering wheel with us (so in his mind he was driving not walking) enabled us to get a lot further.

'When Lee was six months old, he had laryngo-tracheo-bronchitis. He was in and out of hospital over the next six months and on one occasion, nearly died. That was a difficult year. However, over the last thirty-seven years since then, I cannot think of a heartache or pain caused through Lee or his disability.

'I have so many memories of Lee. He was such a joy to bring up; celebrating achievements, birthdays and holidays are particularly good memories and of course, they are still ongoing.

'I like Lee's whole personality; he is affectionate, caring and has a great sense of humour. He is also stubborn and unforgiving at times, but this makes him the unique individual that he is.

'As a child, Lee was extremely good at mimicking and would copy (embarrassingly accurately) the mannerisms etc. of complete strangers. His brother always went upstairs on a bus where possible, to avoid the embarrassments. In church, when I used to preach, Lee would often make comments, especially if he could make people laugh. He also stopped a sermon once given by a preacher we didn't know, by saying "Amen" in a very loud voice, about eight times!

'I am very proud of the independence skills he has developed, which have led to him living in his own flat (with support). I also love his musical conducting skills which give him the *chance to conduct one or two pieces with our band at concerts.*

'I have had no feelings of anger with regard to Lee, unless you include the frustration caused by "professionals" who would not listen to what the mother had to say. My time of "aloneness" came from bringing up both my boys on my own without the support of my husband, but I don't think I've ever felt really alone or lonely.

'My strength has always been, and is, my faith in God. I know that God is always there with me (even though it doesn't always feel like that) and He has always given me the strength to do whatever I have needed to bring my two boys up well.

'I've always received lots of help and support from my friends and sometimes family members. As a child Lee's support from professionals was quite limited, but as an adult both he and I have been supported well and Lee has been, and is, supported to find the lifestyle he now enjoys.

'When Lee was born, expectations of any kind of achievement or independence were severely limited, and I never really expected Lee to have any independence. I am delighted now to see the progress he has made and the independence he's achieved, and to know that his future will continue in a similar way when I am no longer here.'

Anon., 2014c

Our amusing and embarrassing moments

Being a family carer brings all sorts of challenges, and there have been numerous amusing and embarrassing moments of the years. Once our ward clerk at St Catherine's, where I used to work, invited us to the circus which was local to her in Peel Park. It was the first time that Simon had been to the circus, so he was very excited. It was a big top, with wooden benches arranged in tiers around the arena. We enjoyed the performance but as the show progressed, there was bit of a poo noise from Simon...followed by a smell! We realised that there had been some slip-up with toileting; we ignored the smell completely and pretended it wasn't happening. However, as the smell increased, the number of people around us on benches decreased and we were soon isolated! This was probably the least of our problems.

On another occasion Peter took Simon to a meeting where Barbara Castle was speaking (she was a prominent Labour party figure). Fortunately, they sat at the back and luckily, she did not understand that Simon was saying *'rhubarb rhubarb rhubarb!'* However, she was very sweet and came up afterwards and said how good Simon had been.

Family carers' dyslexia

Even though I have done a responsible paid job competently as a registered and specialist nurse, which involved some office work, I now find paperwork difficult to manage and I call this "family carers' dyslexia" but I am not ashamed of it, nor do I apologise for it.

I especially struggle with financial information and Peter, when he has been well enough to do so, has taken control of this.

For me, "family carers' dyslexia" is having to deal with all the paperwork that is sent our way; it is impossible to read it all, digest it all, understand it all and know how to respond. This happens to other family carers too, with people often mentioning how they struggle.

I know that this information affects us significantly, so I am anxious about it and I panic about getting it right; I don't want to make a mistake that could have such a drastic effect. Therefore, I go into a state of panic and often my mind will literally go blank.

Can you imagine having to manage all of these? -

- Care assessments.
- Family carers' assessments.
- Care plans.
- Support agency assessments.
- Support agency support plans.
- Core review documents.
- Disability welfare benefits applications and assessments.

- Contingency plans.
- Life books.
- Timesheets and payroll.
- Organising support, including team meetings, supervisions and training.
- Recruiting new people to support Simon.
- Trustees' documents and holding trustee meetings.
- Medical information.
- Circles of support notes and information.
- Correspondence from social workers, GPs, specialists and the local authority.

I have often thought that official papers, like the accessible guidance papers from the Department of Health, should be published in a manner that is easy to read – no jargon, easy explanations and to the point. When I have seen accessible papers, they are pleasing to the eye, appealing to read, and easier to understand. This principle should be taken into consideration for all information that needs to be shared with family carers.

Then comes the added complication of all the people we have to liaise with, which include:
- Social workers.
- GPs.
- Psychologists.
- Psychiatrists.
- Carers' support workers.
- Speech therapists.
- Tissue viability nurses.
- Support workers.
- Dentists.
- Dieticians.
- Solicitors.
- Circle of support members.
- Trustees.

Then we have to keep up to date with the frequent changes in local and national social care systems, policies, guidance, practices and law! What an awful lot to have to make time to read in an already busy and hectic life.

A small business

The paperwork side of caring (and the wider role of caring) is like running a small business, but I have never received any training or mentoring in doing so, nor have I any interest or inclination towards it. I just want to be a good wife and an even better mother.

Chaos machine

These things are even harder to manage because I am overburdened, which causes me to be a bit scatty. I am forgetful because Simon is a chaos machine with a particular skill for disorientation and requires my full attention. He opens drawers and wardrobes and pulls out the contents, leaving things strewn all over the place. My home is filled with too much stuff which needs sorting out, tidying or disposing of, which I can never get around to doing. If paperwork is left out Simon will tear it up, leaving it in pieces thrown across the floor; he is indiscriminate with it – solicitor's letters under the sofa, bank statements in pieces! I had to have a letter cage fitted to the back of the door, which collects the post; and this is kept locked, so all the post can be kept safe until I have the time to give it some undivided attention, including the junk mail.

Simon likes to have his books and magazines easy to hand; he loves to read his monthly magazines including *Land Rover, Farmer's Weekly, Steam Traction Engines*, and *Flypast*, which often means that the living room floor is covered with them. It is hard to clear things up, as Simon becomes unsettled if he cannot find what he wants – this includes the numerous engines he owns (and the engine drivers), which come in many shapes and sizes. These take up space on the floor and the floors are so covered that we can barely see the carpet.

Make a list

Simon does not understand if you are busy with a task in hand; if he wants your time or attention, for whatever matter, he requires this immediately, making it impossible for me to complete a task. He seeks to completely organise my day with his plans! The only answer to this one is to write out a list together. If Simon can see his request written on paper in a list, it is a big help.

Blitzes and decluttering

I have people in my life who have helped me tremendously and they have been more than willing and happy to come to our home and help with organising and sorting. Without these sessions I would have been very overwhelmed and bogged down. These blitzes include having a general clear-out of old toys and magazines, sorting clothes, filing away paperwork and putting things back in their places around our home.

Precious gift

Simon is a precious gift to me and my husband. We have learnt a great deal from Simon being in our lives and we would not change anything about how our life with him has been. He has taught us about patience, kindness and love and amazes us with the strength he shows every day in his ability to enjoy life and make the most of what is available to him.

He is not a mistake. Simon is a "gift on purpose". He is made in the image of God. As I mentioned earlier, Simon often says, *'Jesus was disabled on the cross.'*

For families who may find themselves in a difficult situation, continue to believe in your child and encourage them to develop. Continue to work towards what is right for them, and ensure you get the outcome that works best for your son or your daughter. It is their future we are shaping, and we need to ensure we make this as secure and enjoyable as possible. Focus on now and on a future where they have a purpose and are appreciated and loved, where they are safe and where their skills, interests and personality shape what their life looks like.

Be proactive for your child and persistent, make the time to network and attend meetings so you can keep up to date with what is going on in the local area and any changes that are taking place. Enlist the support of people and agencies that think outside the box and the same way as you, set up a circle of support, find the things that give you the strength to carry on and keep them close to hand.

Here are some interesting facts and figures about the number of people with a learning disability in the UK

1. There are 13.9 million disabled people in the UK.' (Scope. 2018)

2. In the UK, Mere are tmillion disabled children, 33% more than a decade ago (Disabled Children's Partnership)

3. 99.1 per cent of disabled children live at home and are supported by their families (Contact, the charity for families with disabled children)

4. A quarter of parents of disabled children provide 100 hours of care a week — equivalent to three full- time jobs (Contact research Caring More Than Most 2017)

Walk tall

Through all my experience as a family carer I have learnt to be strong and to "walk tall".

We all face challenges that make us question who we are, the actions we take and the decisions we make. NO MATTER what you are going through at any time of your life, how you are feeling and what you are wearing, stand tall and walk tall.

It doesn't matter if you forget you are wearing carpet slippers, walk tall; you might start a new fashion!

For Christians

For me Jesus gave me faith and strength and If, yourself are religious, remember;

your identity in Christ,

you are a child of the Living God,

you are a channel for the Holy Spirit,

you have been bought with a price (and what a price!!),

with such a glorious identity, we stand tall.

Keep the vision

When times get hard and exhausting, and you do not know where you will find the reserves to deal with the next thing, stop for a second and take stock. Do not let the weight of the world stop you from doing the best that you can for your child. No matter how anyone else views your child, and what they think and say, you remember how wonderful they are and the great times and treasured moments you have had together, because no-one can take that away from you, unless you let them. So, keep the vision and may God bless you.

Sources of useful information

Carers Trust

The Carers Trust network provides support to carers locally across the UK.

Website: https://www.carers.org

Tel: 0300 772 9600

Email: info@carers.org

Carers UK

When caring for a family member or friend, Carers UK is a membership organisation there to provide the support and advice you need to make your life easier. Website: https://www.carersuk.org/

Tel: 020 7378 4999

Email: info@carersuk.org

Citizens Advice

Citizens advice helps give people the knowledge and confidence they need to find their way forward - whoever they are, and whatever their problem. Our network of charities offers confidential advice online, over the phone, and in person, for free. We use our evidence to show big organisations - from companies right up to the government - how they can make things better for people.

Website: https://www.citizensadvice.org.uk

National advice line tel (England): 03444 111 444

Inclusion Network

A network and online hub of resources with the aim of working towards an inclusive society; inspiring and practical ideas to encourage inclusion.

Website: http://www.inclusion.com/

Tel: (416) 658-5363 (head office is based in Toronto, Canada)

E-mail: inclusionpress@inclusion.com

With specific reference to Judith Snow
https://inclusion.com/inclusion-resources/change-makers/

In Control

A national charity working for an inclusive society where everyone has the support they need to live a good life and make a valued contribution.

Website: www.in-control.org.uk

Tel: 0121 474 5900

Email: admi@in-control.org.uk

Mencap Helpline

The Royal Mencap Society is the leading voice of learning disability committed to changing the world for people with a learning disability for the better. Mencap's vision is a world where people who have a learning disability are valued equally, listened to and included.

Mencap's learning disability helpline is a free service providing support and advice for people with a learning disability and their families and carers.

Website: mencap.org.uk/advice-and-support/our-services/learning-disability-helpline

Tel: 0808 808 1111

Email: helpline@mencap.org.uk

National Autistic Society

The National Autistic Society is the UK's leading charity for people. Since 1962, we have been campaigning for autistic people's rights and providing support and advice to autistic people and their families. We are here to transform lives, change attitudes and create a society that works for autistic adults and children.

Website: https://www.autism.org.uk/

Tel: 0808 800 4104

Email: supportercare@nas.org.uk

The Reason I Jump

Using an accessible question and answer format, Naoki Higashida, who has autism, provides a remarkable and rare insight into the mind of a child who has autism. With autism being a spectrum condition that affects everyone differently, there are no set "symptoms" but Higashida, who wrote the book when he was just 13, provides an eye-opening and valuable take on things, making the book one I would highly recommend.

Published by Sceptre and translated by Peter Mitchell, this wonderful book is available to buy on Amazon.co.uk.

References:

Anon., 2014a. *How a student social worker's view on family carers changed in two years after helping me review "Simon's World", spending time with a family carers group, listening to other family carers' accounts of their experiences and gaining insight into my life as a family carer.* [letter] (Personal communication, March 2014)

Anon., 2014b. *Contributions by family carers who are members of Bradford Plan on what it is like to be a family carer – they shared their experiences with me verbally while I wrote what they said down.* [conversation] (Personal communication, March 2014)

Anon., 2014c. *An account from a family carer I know well who told me about her experience caring for a son with a learning disability.* [written] (Personal communication, June 2014)

Carers Trust, 2015a. *About carers.* [online]. Available at: <https://carers.org/what-carer> [Accessed 2 August 2018]

Carers Trust, 2015b. *Key facts about carers and the people they care for.* [online]. Available at: < https://carers.org/key-facts-about-carers-and-people-they-care> [Accessed 3 August 2018] (Old link)

Carer's UK, 2018. *State of Caring 2018.* [pdf] London: Carer's UK. Available at: <https://www.carersuk.org/images/Downloads/SoC2018/State-of-Caring-report-2018.pdf> [Accessed 23 September 2018]

Contact a Family, 2011. *Forgotten Families The impact of isolation on families with disabled children across the UK.* [pdf]. Contact a Family. Available at: <https://contact.org.uk/media/381636/forgotten_isolation_report.pdf> [Accessed 29 November 2018]

Disability Rights UK, 2015. *Personal Budgets: The right social care support.* [online] Available at: <https://www.disabilityrightsuk.org/personal-budgetsthe-right-social-care-support> [Accessed 27 November 2018]

Dundee Carers Centre, 2018. *Dundee Carers Centre.* [online] Available at: <http://dundeecarerscentre.org.uk/about-us> [Accessed 18 September 2018]

Elwell, L., 2018. *Rights of Passage.* Worcestershire: In Control

Getty, K. and Townend, S., 2002. *Lord of Every Heart.* [CD] Kingsway Music

Inclusion Europe, n.d. *Relationship map.* [image online] Available at: <http://www.inclusion-europe.com/topside/en/site_content/81-person-centred-planning-tools-eg-passion-audit-relationship-map/244-circles-of-support> [Accessed 25 August 2018]

Kirkham, J., 2011. *Discussion in which insight was gained from a support worker who had worked with Simon for a number of years on how some of the day-to-day tasks that can be taken for granted in other people's lives can be incredibly difficult for the person who is cared for and the family.* [conversation] (Personal communication, n.d. 2011)

Mencap, 2006. *Breaking Point – families still need a break.* [pdf] London: Mencap. Available at: <https://www.mencap.org.uk/sites/default/files/2016-07/Breaking%20Point%20Families_still_need_a_break%202006.pdf> [Accessed 23 September 2018]

National Autistic Society, 2016. *Autism.* [online] Available at: <https://www.autism.org.uk/about/what-is/asd.aspx> [Accessed 18 September 2018]

Nicholson, W., 2014. *Community Nursing Supporting the health and wellbeing of carers across the life course.* [pdf]. Department of Health. Available at: <https://professionals.carers.org/sites/default/files/9._supporting_the_health_and_wellbeing_of_carers_0.pdf> [Accessed 18 September 2018]

O'Leary, M., 2017. Caring Choices. *Choices,* (99), p.2

Scope, 2018. Disability facts and figures. [online] Available at: <https://assets.publishing.service.gov.uk/government/uploads/system/uploads/attachment_data/file/692771/family-resources-survey-2016-17.pdf> [Accessed 13 September 2020]

Thompson, 2018a. *Discussion about how, as family carers, the phrase "look after yourself" makes us feel.* [conversation] (Personal communication, n.d. 2018)

Thompson, 2018b. *An account of a carer's experience dealing with social services and the council.* [written] (Personal communication, n.d. 2018)

Lightning Source UK Ltd.
Milton Keynes UK
UKHW021825080522
402647UK00005B/151